LEVEL UP:

Entrepreneur Spirit Blueprint

By Vita Ann

Cover design by Minor Production
IG: @minorproduction007

TABLE OF CONTENTS

Level Up: Entrepreneur Spirit Blueprint

DEDICATION

This book is dedicated to all my dreamers and doers. If you can see it and say it, you can execute and build it. Never let anyone rob you of your happiness and dreams. Brace yourself as you enter the entrepreneur spirit because your life will never be the same! So, get ready to create your legacy because it will look nothing like your past.

Level Up: Entrepreneur Spirit Blueprint

CHAPTER 1

WHAT IS AN ENTREPRENEUR?

"Everyone can tell you the risk, an entrepreneur can see the reward."

-Robert Kiyosaki

An entrepreneur is an insane person who is crazy enough to risk everything they own, including their health, to create a business. Just joking. I figured I would use my sense of humor to break the ice because you are not supposed to be nervous entering the entrepreneur world. It's a ride you will never forget, and by the time you finish reading this book you will be sharp as a razor, equipped with the skills needed to become a successful entrepreneur and/or determine if this is the right journey for you. Entrepreneurship is not for everyone so this book will outline whether you are walking the right path or not.

Truthfully speaking, from my experience, the worst thing you could do is waste time fulfilling the wrong purpose. Trust me, I know. I have certifications and background skills in many industries. Now, I'm not saying it's a bad thing because it's always a plus to have as much under your belt as possible. Every credential counts and I will show you why it's beneficial in a later chapter. I have many trades on my resume from trying to figure out my passion and purpose, which we will also discuss in a later chapter on how to distinguish between, purpose, passion, and talents. You can't get wasted time back and of course we all know timing is everything, and money is time. But back to the million-dollar question: what is an entrepreneur?

"An entrepreneur is a person who organizes and operates a business or businesses, taking on greater than normal financial risks in order to do so." In other words, an entrepreneur is someone who puts in blood, sweat, and tears to make their dreams come true. I have heard many stories from successful people on their journey and what it took for them to get to the top and the sacrifices that they had to make. One thing you must realize is that entrepreneurs make many sacrifices big sacrifices. Understand that sometimes you have to take one step back to get ten steps ahead. Think of all the stories from your favorite celebrities and people you look up to that are successful. They went through hell and back and faced some of the most horrible struggles that you probably can't even imagine. From losing everything, to being homeless, to putting their all into their dreams, and being turned down a million times. Many entrepreneurs have been flat broke before they made it big. But they still managed to keep their faith alive because they believed in themselves as well as their vision and wouldn't accept "no" for an answer. They stayed persistent, consistent, and knew that their day would come but they had to wait their turn.

Do you really know how hard it is to be an entrepreneur? From swallowing your pride, to faking it until you make it, to people looking down upon you and judging you while you're walking your path, and even holding you to certain expectations, forcing you to consistently wear a mask and show no signs of weakness. No matter what, you're never supposed to let them see you sweat. You just don't hear many entrepreneurs talking about it because entrepreneurs don't complain. They understand that if they stay true to their blueprint then they will see the light at the end of the tunnel exactly how they envisioned it to be. They know in the end they will have victory. An entrepreneur is someone who is willing to risk and sacrifice everything, such as a stable job, family, friends, health, and free time. Whatever it takes, entrepreneurs are up for the challenge. An entrepreneur is very humble and doesn't work with pride. What's pride when you're trying to make it to the top? That's the mindset that you have to have when being an entrepreneur. "Pride comes before the fall." An entrepreneur is someone who is a visionary and sees the big picture. For example, think of the way a hair stylist sees the finished hairstyle before they start. The same is true for an entrepreneur. They see the business concept and how it fits in the economy before it is complete, which is one of their many gifts. They are very good at painting pictures without a paint brush and paper.

I remember when I launched my first book, *#1 Rule: Never Give Up*, which is based on true events, I took my last bit of money to launch my book. I literally had to rob Peter to pay Paul. I had to give up everything just so I could solely focus on launching my book. I owed money to the bank, I was behind in bills. I was willing to lose it all to win again because I knew the potential my book had if I could launch it successfully, so that's what I did. I took a risk that forever changed my life. (You check read that book to learn more about my life and struggles.) I have come a long way.

Keep in mind that after you get your business off the ground you can't just think money is going to come pouring in like a fountain, because that's not realistic. It can happen, but it's rare. To be an entrepreneur you have to be ready to walk through Hell before you get to Heaven and face failure firsthand. before we go any further please realize there is no shortcut to success. You must put in the foot work or else success will never come knocking at your door. When you launch your first business you enter the boxing ring and that's when the real fight begins. Later down the line it will get easier as you grow and learn from trial and error. Take me for example. The first year, book sales were slow because I was pushing and doing everything myself. I couldn't afford to pay to have a business team. But the lessons and connections I gained from putting in that foot work were priceless, and guess what? I weathered the storm, went broke, barely could survive, and finally my breakthrough came. Hard work definitely pays off. You just have to be patient and appreciate the journey, both the ups and downs.

Choosing to be an entrepreneur is one of the hardest things to do, but the best decision that you could ever make. To be an entrepreneur you have to have tough skin, you have to be willing to accept a million NOs before you get that one YES that will change your life forever. You have to be strong enough to realize that it is your dream, it is your vision, it is your responsibility to make your dream become a reality and nobody else's. Don't get upset or discouraged when people, including close friends and loved ones, don't share the same passion about whatever venture you are about to take on. Don't get upset when you don't get the right support needed to help your business succeed. And always remember, many people will not support nor believe in your vision or dream until it is already successful and off the ground. That is just the reality of it. When you do find people who believe in you, hold on to them tight because you will need them, trust me. They will be your cheerleaders cheering you on when you're having those dark moments and are ready to give up. They will give you the extra boost of energy that you need to keep fighting. Also, keep in mind it is your duty to keep that dream alive, but be thankful for the ones that do believe and support you along this crazy journey that you're about to take on. What's for you is for you and when you feel like it is your turn, take it and run with it. Don't let anyone talk you out of your dreams because you don't know the "why" behind their reasons. Entrepreneurship is not for everyone. "Entrepreneurship is not a part-time job, and it's not even a full-time job. It's a lifestyle."-Carrie Layne

To be an entrepreneur you must be a risk taker. But everyone is not a risk taker and they will give you advice to help you play it safe from their point of view. The worst thing you can do is flush your dreams down the toilet because of the energy and advice you let others instill in you, but that will come in a later chapter about the mindset needed to survive as an entrepreneur. Remember tough times don't last but tough people do. You are in a race where if you don't make your dreams a reality then eventually your dreams will become someone else's. Being an entrepreneur you have to be willing to be the only person running all aspects of the business until you can afford to hire help, so prepare to have sleepless nights, anxiety, tears, and the feeling of wanting to give up.

The worst thing you can do is give up on your dreams because once you do that you are giving up on yourself, second guessing your potential, and if you don't believe in yourself how can you expect others to believe in you? You have to fight, fight, fight for your place in the entrepreneur world. The effort that you put in determines how successful your business venture will be. What you put in is what you get back. Don't worry or panic. I did a lot of the hard work for you.

One of my reasons for wanting to write this book was because I know many people dream of being their own boss, but just don't know how to properly execute it. I want to help your dreams become reality. Look, we all have a purpose and the potential to make anything happen. We are the smartest creatures on this earth. We, as humans, built the pyramids, houses, cars, bridges, you name it. Everything that is on this earth we built, so don't ever think that it's impossible. We have the power to make the impossible possible. When you are thinking about your dreams it should give you some type of bubbly feeling. Entrepreneurs are opportunists in a good way. If it makes sense and it makes money, then we will find a way to make it a reality. Entrepreneurs are people who are doers, and not big on hoping, waiting, or wishing. Entrepreneurs are not just in one industry They can bounce around in any industry because they have the skills and mindset to learn any industry. Entrepreneurship is very hard but the satisfaction that you can gain from the finished business venture is indescribable. You can create your own legacy for many generations after you.

CHAPTER 2

WHAT IS THE ENTREPRENEUR SPIRIT?

So now that we have a clear understanding of what an entrepreneur is, let's look into what the entrepreneur spirit is. To be a true entrepreneur you have to be able to adopt both entrepreneurship and the entrepreneur spirit. The entrepreneur spirit is a mindset. Think of the entrepreneur spirit as the Holy Ghost of the business world. Now, wait, I know it sounds crazy but let me break it down. The entrepreneur spirit is a set of beliefs and values that entrepreneurs believe in, and it's something they practice on a daily basis. Let's take a Christian, for example. They study the Bible and make it a part of their daily life to educate them on the evolution of the world, how it was created, and what is needed to be a good-hearted human being. They hope that by following the Bible it will lead them to the heavenly gates of everlasting life. Also, they go to church and surround themselves with like-minded people who are trying to reach the same goals. By adopting the right mindset, belief system, and being the best Christian possible they know that in the end they will catch the Holy Ghost, live righteous, have a better chance of making it to heaven, and be cleansed of their sins. They are that much closer to God.

Now the same is true for the entrepreneur spirit. Entrepreneurs adopt a certain mindset and belief system, gain knowledge by reading books, and surround ourselves with like-minded people by engaging in events and gatherings. If you continuously network with successful people, nine times out of ten you will begin to follow and adopt their habits. You can gain the entrepreneur spirit and increase your chances of becoming a successful individual and having your dreams come true. Entrepreneurs are like sponges; they soak up all types of knowledge because they understand the power in knowledge.

Entrepreneurs daydream about financial freedom and the good life. They don't want a normal career. They dream of, after all their hard work, the house on the hills, freedom, a luxurious life, the lives and environment they will be able to change. They have a different mindset and beliefs than the average person. They live life on the edge. Entrepreneurs are the type of people who jump out of an airplane and build a parachute on the way down because they know the bigger the risk the bigger the reward. They run towards risks while others shy away from them. Anything entrepreneurs do they give it 150% of their all. It's either go hard or not at all. Entrepreneurs love challenges. The one thing I love most about entrepreneurs is they see potential in people even when people don't see it in themselves. They love to inspire people and build more leaders to be the best that they can be. Entrepreneurs have a way of pulling the best out of people. They love bringing out the greater good in people and helping people whenever they have the capabilities. Entrepreneurs love being the hero and saving or changing people's lives. On the flip side, entrepreneurs hate wasting their time and hate when others waste their time too, because they have everything planned to the T and can't afford distractions. Entrepreneurs are always staying up to date on the latest trends and news. They're always going to social gatherings for a chance to network and gain more contacts, possible clients, and more exposure. Entrepreneurs never give up on their dreams, no matter how long it will take to make their dreams a reality.

To sum it up, an entrepreneur's job is to pave the way and get others to believe and follow suit. Entrepreneurs create new potential profits as well as open new markets. They are the problem solvers for the economy. Entrepreneurs get a rush out of turning nothing into something. Most importantly. entrepreneurs trust their instinct. They will take advice and love seeking others' opinions even when their mind made up because they value different points of view. Now, take a deep breath.

Maybe take a little break and gather your thoughts to make sure we are still on the same page. Go get yourself a nice little snack or maybe a glass of wine to relax you because this only the beginning. Use the break to digest what you've learned thus far. Remember, it's your race, your pace. Trust the process and don't rush it. I want you to get this down pat. I believe in you and I know you can do it. I know some of you may be nervous and/or overwhelmed, but I promise that you will be just fine. I will be with you every step of the way. I created a bulletproof plan for you that I've used along my journey that got me to where I am today. I can't wait to hear all of your success stories.

Level Up: Entrepreneur Spirit Blueprint

CHAPTER 3

DEFINE YOUR WHY

"The worst kind of sad is not being able to explain why."

Now that we got that covered the definitions of an entrepreneur and the entrepreneur spirit, let's talk about what you need to know before entering the entrepreneur spirt. What is your why behind it? Why do you want to be an entrepreneur? This a very important question and this will determine how strong your foundation will be because a strong foundation is built from your why. This will determine your drive. This will determine how hungry you are for success. So, ask yourself this question: why do you want to be your own boss? Are you just looking to gain some extra money? Is this a part-time thing or full-time thing? Did you always want to be an entrepreneur? This is where you have to dig deep within yourself to find your why.

Let's start with me. I dreamed of owning my own business since I was about seven years old. But as I got older, I really set it in stone and got to the bottom of why I wanted to be an entrepreneur. For one, I wanted to be my own boss because of the freedom it allows you to have and I wanted to be financially free. I wanted to create residual income because the worst thing you can do is stress about how you will survive and feel unsure what the future holds for you. I wanted to give my family a good life without having to worry about how we would pay bills and afford to go on family trips. I wanted to make sure my children's future was secure.

People say money is not everything and I totally agree, but money can ease a lot of stress. Money can guarantee you a stable life, home, and happiness for you and your family. It can help you put your children into a good college to secure their future. It can help you plan for your retirement, because who knows what will happen with Social Security, and if it will be around when you get ready to retire? A good rule of thumb is to never put your eggs all in one basket. Invest in different retirement plans such as a 401(k), simple IRA, and Roth IRA. There are several other retirement plans, each offering different benefits. You just have to figure out which best fits you and your needs. Without money it can be difficult to enjoy life. This is a big earth but if you don't have the money, health, or freedom, you will never be able to explore such a beautiful world. There are roughly 195 different countries in the world today and many people will never get a chance to leave their country. Can you imagine traveling to different countries and islands, exploring the world? Many people only get to see a small speck of the world. There are so many different things to explore in this world that many will never know exist. Amazing tropical islands and resorts. You have one life to live and you should live it to the fullest. Some people say money is the root of all evil, but it's really greed that is the root of all evil. So, don't ever feel bad about securing your future financially for you and your loved ones. If you don't, who will?

I didn't ever want to be a work slave. I figured why bust my booty helping someone else get rich when I can invest in myself and create my own company? I just refused to do that. Also, I have a problem with control and authority over my life. I don't need anyone telling me when I have to work, when I can take a vacation, and mostly importantly, how much my labor is worth. That is just a big problem for me. I never wanted to work until I'm 50-60 years old for someone else. I also want to retire comfortably. I want to expand my capabilities. I know I wasn't put on this earth to just work, retire, and die. Since I was a kid, I always knew there was so much more to life than what I was seeing. I always was curious as to why I was put on this earth. I knew I had a purpose and I as I got older, I discovered it. "The future belongs to the curious. The ones who are not afraid to try it, explore it, poke at it, question it and turn it inside out." I want to make as much money as I want to and not have to worry about how I am going to buy luxurious things and have an enjoyable life. I want happiness and peace, and the only way I can have that is if I am financially free. So, I realized I needed to be my own boss. That's the only way I can truly live life. That's when I decided that being an entrepreneur was my only way to have everything that life has to offer me.

I also wanted to be able to change other people's lives. I want to help others be financially free or at least achieve some financial ease. That's why I'm writing this book. We all have the power to be our own boss so why sell yourself short? There is so much money in the world and there's no reason why everyone cannot have a happy and abundant life. My health is very important to me and stress causes all types of diseases. I never wanted to stress over money! And no one has to because there are many ways to get it. You can live the life that you have always imagined. Have you ever watched TV and seen the lifestyles of the rich and famous and wished you could have houses, cars, and vacations like they have? Have you ever thought *if only I had money, I could do these things*? The only thing that comes to a sleeper is a dream.

Why dream when you can create greatness?

You can create your legacy and it can be there well after you exit this earth for the next generation and for your loved ones. That's another reason why I choose to be an entrepreneur. I want to be remembered as a creator, as a builder, as somebody who made a positive impact in this world. I want to be known as a leader and that is a big part of being an entrepreneur. Those are my reasons why I choose to be an entrepreneur. So, tell me your reason! What is your why? Why do you want to be an entrepreneur? Why do you want to take this path? Your why will be the building blocks for your company. It will be the drive that you need to keep pushing through the dark moments way before you even see the light at the end of the tunnel. Your why will be the reason that you keep getting in the ring and keep fighting. Your why is the reason you will not be defeated by life or by anything that is thrown your way as you walk the path of entrepreneurship. So please take some time to define your why because this is the core to your future.

There is a why behind everything that you do in life. For example, let's say you want to buy a new car but don't have all the money. What you do? You go to work and do overtime and work more than your normal hours until you meet your goal of getting that brand-new car. You don't stop working overtime no matter how tired you get, no matter how many days you have to work. Your desire for the new car is the why behind you working all those long hours. The same is applied when being an entrepreneur. You make sacrifices such as working two jobs, moving in with someone, going to school, investing all your money into your company, educating yourself, welcoming change because of your why of owing your own company, being your own boss, and having the life you always wanted.

Now also, make sure that this is something that you really want to do, because there is no turning back once you've invested so much of your time, money, and energy. What I suggest you do is get a piece of paper and write why you want to be an entrepreneur and why you think that people should believe in you and follow your lead. What are you going to do to add value to the world? How are you going to make a difference? This is the first step to create your greatness. Because people decide to be an entrepreneur for different reasons. Some choose to be one because they are looking for a side hustle, and others have hobbies that they are good at and want to earn some extra cash from. Some are in it for the long haul and want to be a full-time entrepreneur. Answering these questions and discovering your why will help you determine how deep you want to go into being an entrepreneur. You must be real with yourself. It's fine if you want to be a part-time entrepreneur you might be content with your career and just would like to make some extra cash on the side. That's fine. I just want you to know what it means to be a true entrepreneur.

You have entrepreneurs and then you have hustlers. Many people confuse entrepreneurs with hustlers. Know the difference! A hustler is someone who has a good product or service and is just looking to make a come up and make some extra money. Entrepreneurs are trying to build a brand from scratch. So first figure out if you are an entrepreneur or if you are looking for a hustle to make some extra cash. I would hate for you to waste your time to finally figure out this path is not for you. This book is created for those who want to be their own boss and are ready to be a true entrepreneur. Hopefully, I didn't overwhelm you or come down too hard, but I really want you to get it right. I am passionate about helping others find their purpose and bring out their inner entrepreneur. I know you can do it so consider this a little tough love for your future. Now after you write your why behind wanting to be an entrepreneur you have to determine if your whys are strong enough for you to keep going. Is your why worth all the blood, sweat, and tears that you will shed? Is your why stronger than the sacrifices you are about to be make? Most importantly, make sure it is *your* why and not someone else's. You should never walk into someone else's shadow. "You can copy all you want, but you will always be one step behind." You should only walk your path, so make sure your why is truly genuine and authentic. Don't do something because you see someone else doing it because you will be disappointed in the end. What is for you is for you and no nobody else. Take some time. Don't rush your why list. Sit back and reflect on it. You may need to take a couple days and let it sink in a little.

Now if your why is strong enough, congratulations! Welcome to the gates of entrepreneurship! I am super proud of you. Now things are about to get heated up and we are about to get down to the good stuff, so, let the lessons begin! Make sure you have your pen and notebook ready to take notes. I want you to be able to retain this good information I am about to pass on to you. Consider yourself lucky because I created less stairs for you to walk up but am still making sure you take the steps. You still have to face some of your own challenges. I am just going to take a little pressure off of you. Keep your why list somewhere safe so you can always go back and reflect on it when times get rough. There is nothing like a solid reminder to help you keep pushing forward.

Level Up: Entrepreneur Spirit Blueprint

CHAPTER 4

PROS AND CONS OF BEING AN EMPLOYEE

"Customers will never love a company until the employees love it first."

-Simon Sinek

Entrepreneurship is not for everyone and sometimes the benefits of being a well-paid employee for a company outweigh being an entrepreneur. For many it seems like a better opportunity. Just like some people dream of being an entrepreneur, many dream of landing their dream job and working for a big well-known company. Many dream of being a CEO of a well-established company. Many understand their role and prefer to run and manage an already established company versus starting one from scratch and having to worry about the headaches that entrepreneurship brings. Again, everything is not for everybody. I outlined a few pros and cons of being an employee, but the decision is ultimately yours, so choose wisely.

Pros of Being an Employee

First on the list is a paycheck. No matter what happens with the company you are for certain that you can expect a paycheck on pay day, which is a big stress reliever. For example, let's say there are some malfunctions that the company is experiencing that have nothing to do with you; you can still expect to get a paycheck, as long as you have worked your scheduled hours. Lots of people play it safe and choose to be an employee because of the guaranteed check that they will receive every pay period. Another plus is that if you work over a certain number of hours per week you can get paid time and a half. For instance, if you work over 40 hours within the pay week, after you exceed those 40 hours most employers have to pay you time and a half according to the law. So, instead of getting paid $12 an hour you will be paid

$18 an hour after you go over your 40 hours. Nice, right?

Another perk is that you get paid time off, such as vacation time and sick days…and you can still count on receiving a paycheck. Your mind can be more at ease when you don't have to worry about where your next client or money is coming from. You don't have to worry about if it is going to be a slow week or not. That is the company's job, not yours, which takes a lot of stress and pressure off of you. Another pro is not having to worry about health insurance premiums. This is an especially good perk in the United States where health insurance can be very expensive. Also, some companies will even match your retirement plan, and some will pay for you to further your education. Now that's a major plus. Also, the chain of command is already set in stone and your job duties and responsibilities are already established so you don't have to worry about pop up surprises or what you have to tackle for the day to keep the company running. All you have to do is your assigned job, leave, and go on with your day to day life after your shift is over. You don't have to take your work life problems home. Once your shift is done then you can go home and continue your everyday personal life with your family and friends.

Taxes, taxes, taxes. We can avoid a lot of things in life, but we can't avoid Uncle Sam. Uncle Sam always wants his piece of the pie for sure. Being an employee, you don't have to worry about certain taxes, such as self-employee tax, estimated tax, and other taxes which can be pretty steep. I mean as an employee you still have to pay taxes, but you also qualify for refundable tax credit, which is how you get a tax refund check after January. So, consider yourself lucky because while your employer has to pay taxes, after January you get a nice little check which can range from $500-$10,000 every year, depending on what you put down on your w-4 form and your qualifying dependents. Nice, right? Then you can put that check into your savings account, invest, or even take a nice trip every year. Furthermore, a major plus is that with the right college credentials, experience, and effort you can easily move up within the company. This means you become more of an asset to the company and can get an increase in pay. To sum this up, the pros of being an employee are that you provide your labor and time for a stable paycheck, and still walk away with lots of beneficial perks while your boss carries on the headache of having to make sure the company grows and thrives enough to cover all the expenses and hopefully after it's done have some profits left. Business owners get paid last while staff get paid first.

Cons of Being an Employee

One of the biggest cons of being an employee is that you may not get paid what you really are worth. The company has a budget and sets their pay rates according to what they feel their workers deserve to be paid. You may have to work overtime just to compensate for what you feel you should be bringing home. Also, you cannot control your destiny within the company. You can be working one day and laid off or fired the next. No matter how long or hard you have worked for that company, at the end of the day your boss gets the final say. In addition, not everyone likes their boss/manager. There are some really good bosses, but then there are some micromanaging bosses who are always looking over your shoulder to see how well you're doing your job and criticizing you to try to get you to do it better. Your job can make changes without your approval, and you have no choice but to adjust to the change or find another job. They may ship you to a different department without your input. Due to expansion your duties, as well as team members, may change, and there is nothing you can do about it. You can voice your opinion, but that does not mean anything is going to change. And your work schedule may not be fixed. You may work first shift for one week and second shift the following week if the company feels as though they want their workers to routinely change shifts. It may not always be a bad thing. Some people like changing shifts because it gives you a chance to switch job responsibilities and not get bored doing the same thing over and over again every day, which can be very tedious.

Lastly, you may find it hard to follow your passions when putting in so many work hours. You will be drained and once your shift over is and you're dealing with your personal life, following your passion may be the last thing on your mind. All you will want to do is go home, relax, and prepare for the next workday. You can get so wrapped up at the work place the next thing you know you've been with the company for 10-20 years, and your passion and dreams are out the door because you've put so much time into someone else's company, helping them grow their enterprise that you forget to build and grow your own. Can you imagine living your whole life and retiring and not having any legacy to leave behind but being a hard worker for a company and maybe retiring comfortably? You probably wouldn't even get the right recognition for all your hard work.

CHAPTER 5
PROS AND CONS OF BEING AN ENTREPRENEUR

"I'd rather hustle 24/7 than slave 9-5."

Now that you know the pros and cons of being an employee let's discuss the ups and downs of being an entrepreneur. First and foremost, being an entrepreneur, you are your own boss. It's your race at your own pace. You dictate when, where, why, and how your company moves. You have total control over all the important decision making to utilize your skills and strengths to your full potential. Furthermore, the excitement that entrepreneurs get from building nothing to something is amazing because every day they face a different challenge and new opportunities. It is like going on a different adventure every day. Pretty cool, right? Another pro is being able to work in an industry that is your passion, meaning you have a chance to turn your passion to profits, so it doesn't ever feel like work. Unfortunately, when being a worker most of the time, you work at a workplace for the pay and not the passion, which makes it so much harder.

Freedom is one of the major reasons why many people choose to be an entrepreneur. Freedom allows you to work when you want to and take off or take a break as you please. Not to mention the profits that you make from being an entrepreneur. The work and effort that you put out determines the profits that you bring in. Can you imagine making as much money as you want to? You know the saying: "Hard work pays off." Entrepreneurs live by that, and that's why most entrepreneurs work extra hard. Because they plan or cashing out even harder. Flexibility is also another perk of being an entrepreneur because you can work around your own schedule however you choose to. For example, if you were a college student and thinking about going full-time, let's say 3-4 times a week, then you can work around your school schedule, which is always a plus. Entrepreneurs believe that chances make champions, and the rewards and profits are far greater than the risk. Once you become an entrepreneur and your business venture becomes a success, freedom comes with it. Entrepreneurs set their own schedule and pick when they want to work. Entrepreneurs work really hard but can also play even harder. Entrepreneurs may work hard for long extended periods of time, barely eating healthy, barely sleeping, just to execute a venture but once it's done, we can travel, shop, or relax for as long as we please! We can even sleep as long as we want to so it all balances out in the end.

Cons of Being an Entrepreneur

Being an entrepreneur can be mentally, financially, and emotionally stressful at times, and can also have long-term health effects. That's what makes entrepreneurs special kinds of people, because they risk so much. First, let's be clear; once you are an entrepreneur and running your own business you will never leave work. Yes, even when you go on vacations your phone will never stop ringing. You just have to find a way to balance it out, such as maybe leaving someone in charge when you plan on taking a vacation. It is like having a child. Your job is never done, no matter what. This can put extra stress on you because it takes you away from your loved ones, friends, and could even cause problems if you have a significant other. Also, be aware it might not be lucrative at first and you may not see a paycheck for long periods of time. Way before money comes rolling in you will more than likely have financial problems and be in debt, so always make sure you have a little cushion before stepping into the entrepreneur world. I will discuss that in a later chapter about ways to ease your stress and save for rainy days. I found a blueprint to counteract a lot of problems that many entrepreneurs face on their journey.

Also, many entrepreneurs can stress so much at the beginning it can cause problems like anxiety, depression, and mood swings. The key is to be strong mentally because entrepreneurs have to be willing to adjust to change, which starts mentally. You will fail many times and you have to be quick on your feet so you can bounce back. If not, you will take your failures hard, making it hard to keep pushing forward. Another con of being an entrepreneur is that you will have to run all aspects of the business. You will be in charge of everything as your company continues to grow, until you can afford to pay a staff. You can, however, always try to look for volunteers to help do some work too. So be ready and put your boxing gloves on because you will be in for a fight. Don't worry, though. This is only the beginning it definitely gets greater later.

Another con is finding people to help grow your vision who are just as excited about the business venture as you are. Remember, teamwork makes the dream work so make sure your team is strong and had one common goal. Many people start a business and want to bring family members and friends aboard because they feel as though they deserve a position within your company because they are your loved ones.

That's not always a good idea. They may mean well but may not go as hard for your vision because you all may not share a common goal. So, proceed with caution when hiring help and make sure your help will assist you in meeting your end goal. In addition to that, being the boss, you have to pay all the overhead costs, such as employee wages, insurance, taxes, office space, etc. These expenses can add up to a pretty ugly bill depending on the company size and category. To sum this up, the major disadvantages of being an entrepreneur are that you take on all risks, including financial, and you are the only one held accountable. When it's going well you take the credit and when it's bad you must be willing to take credit too. Look at the whole Covid-19 pandemic and how one minute businesses were thriving and then the next minute companies were forced to shut down and lay off workers or still run their businesses at a slower pace and still have to pay their workers. Even though business owners got assistance, for some it wasn't enough, which is why some were forced to shut down.

Risks like this comes with being a business owner. You will have endless responsibility. People will depend on you so that they have a way to feed their families so running a tight ship is ideal. You make scarifies and have to be very disciplined and carry the most weight. It can trigger health issues from all the pressure that comes along with it, so sit back for a minute and ask yourself are you willing to take on all the loads just to be your own boss?

It's decision and reflection time! Now that we've taken a look into the pros and cons of being an employee versus an entrepreneur, hopefully you've decided that the entrepreneur path is for you. Once you make that decision it is time for you to adapt a new mindset for your new beginning because, trust me, you will need it to be a successful entrepreneur. You are about to dig even deeper within yourself so get ready!

Level Up: Entrepreneur Spirit Blueprint

CHAPTER 6

NEW MINDSET, NEW BEGINNING

"Life isn't about finding yourself. It is about creating yourself."

- George Bernard Shaw

"The secret of change is to focus all of your energy, not on fighting the old, but on building the new."

-Socrates

In order to achieve greatness and be an entrepreneur you must be equipped with the right state of mind. You have to be strong. But first you have to choose to change. So, in this chapter we are going to be discussing what a healthy non-toxic mind is like, and how to reprogram your mind. "You're always one decision away from a totally different life." Old habits won't open new doors. Old habits will have you reopening the same doors. Growth is very painful because that's when you get a chance to dig deep within yourself and within others around you. This is when you realize what is healthy for you and what is poison for you. This is the stage where you will remove unwanted things in your life, such as habits and people, even family and friends. Just remember, people are in your life for a reason or a season. Not everyone will make it to the end of the tunnel with you. This is where you are about to make your biggest sacrifices because it is never easy letting go of things and people that you thought had your best interest at heart. This where you are going to have to let go of a lot of things, so prepare yourself. This is where you will discover what state of mind you are currently in. It doesn't matter if your life is a total mess. Never think it is too late for you to change. As long as you are still six feet above and not six feet under then you have a chance to reinvent yourself. So, don't look at how far you have to go. Look at how far you've already come and the greatness that you will create once you decide to change.

The first step to change is to never play the victim. You have to take accountability for your life, your decisions, and situations that you placed yourself in. Also, never complain. You made certain decisions which placed you where you are today. Whether good or bad, you did it! Too often people complain about why their life is not going the way they want it to go. We have all played the victim before. You have to break your old cycles to get a different outcome. You have to be willing pick your life apart to figure out where you went wrong so you know what not to do when it's time to build it back up. There is nothing more stressful than repeating the same mistake over and over again. That is what you call an insane person. Ask yourself this question: are you playing the victim in your current life? If so, why? What makes you think you are the victim? And if so, what are you going to do to change that? I hope you survive and thrive from it! Are you ready to remove yourself from that victim status to victory status? Are you truly ready to change? "Don't be a victim of yourself. Forget about the thief waiting in the alley; what about the thief in your mind?" – Jim Rohn

Secondly, you have to be tired of being sick of tired. Have you ever been so tired of something that one day you say *enough! I can't do this anymore*? That's the attitude you have to have with your mind. You can't allow your thoughts to run your life anymore. You can't allow certain situations and decisions to run your life anymore. You can't keep living in your past. In order to change YOU have to want it; nobody else. I can want you to change all day, which I do because everyone has greatness inside of them and it saddens me when people don't realize that. But if you're not ready then you're just not ready. It took me years to get it right and guess when I got it? When I hit rock bottom. Sometimes it takes for you to lose everything to win again, but what I realized is that nobody on this earth can want it for you more than you want it for yourself. You have to put that energy out into the universe so that energy in turn can invite change. Just like the work that you put out will determine your level of success as an entrepreneur, the same is true for your mind. The energy and effort that you put into things and your mindset will determine your inner growth as a person.

Also, you have to know when to remove people who don't mean you well out of your life, whether it is family members or friends. If they're not helping you grow as a person, why surround yourself around them? The purpose of having people in your life is so they can add to your happiness and growth, not take it away. Don't feel bad about cutting people off if they do not feel bad about seeing you struggle and not grow. On my journey to a new mindset I had to cut so many people out of my life that I thought meant me good. I started to pick my life apart and that's when I realized some people that were in my life could be silent killers of your future. Now I'm not saying that all the people in your life may be out to get you or have a grudge against you. I'm just saying many may not be striving for what you are striving for. Their point of view may be different from your point of view and you may have to love them from a distance. On the other hand, some people that are in your life really don't mean you well. I have had people sit front row just waiting for me to fail. So, you really have to watch out for the fake help and love because some people do have hidden agendas. One thing about time is that it always reveals the truth, whether you want to face it or not. Have you ever heard the saying "Hang around nine broke people and you will be the tenth broke person"? Consider that every time you invite people into your life. Will you be the tenth broke person hanging around them? Will you be the tenth person who can't seem to get it right? Will you be the tenth person to live without change? Will you be the tenth to not serve your purpose in life? Ask yourself what you will be the tenth of. Before we go any further, let's take a little break and do an exercise.

Grab a pen and paper and write down how you currently view your life. What are the good things in your life? What are the bad things in your life? Then get another piece of paper and write down the people that you have in your life. Write them all down. The order does not matter. Just get their names down on paper. Next to each name describe them as a person and describe what they add to your life. Now after doing this list, write a check mark next to the names of all the people who add value and happiness to your life. The ones who are rooting for your success and want to see you do well.

For the names left without a check mark, write down their relationship to you, how you met them, and their current life status. Afterwards, ask yourself why you have these toxic people in your life. What makes you think they deserve to be in your life and why do you think they will bring you any good if they have nothing good going for themselves? Finally, ask yourself what's holding you back from cutting them out of your life, or from just loving them from a distance. "Sometimes you have to love people from a distance and give them the space and time to get their minds right before you let them back into your life." - Robert Tew.

This is the part where your eyes are going to be wide open and this is where you need to do some rearranging of your environment to welcome change. I'm pretty sure we all have family members that we love dearly but just can't deal with for whatever reason. You have to remove the bad out of your life and make room for the good. That's the only way you can change and evolve as a person. Another thing you must realize is that misery loves company. Watch out for those wolves in sheep's clothing because there are a lot of them walking around this earth, and sometimes they are the people closest to you. So, be careful who you invite into your life and make sure they mean you well. People came into my life that I thought had my back and best interest at heart and they turned around and hurt me the most. But remember when people do bad stuff to you, you truly have to forgive them and move on. "Never block your blessings trying to teach somebody a lesson." The best revenge you can give someone is to move on without them stealing your joy, no matter what they did to you. "Success is the best revenge." There were so many times I wanted to get payback on people that hurt me, but when I sat back and thought about it, I realized I would not be proving anything by paying them back. They were already going to get paid back by me simply removing them from my life and showing them that they are no longer welcomed in my space.

Now that we've covered that, there is a cure to all of this! Once you remove those toxic people you have to know how to deal with everything moving forward. I learned and mastered it. Have you ever heard of dharma? It is the opposite of karma. Just like karma comes back when you do bad things, dharma is the good you have done coming back to you. For example, karma is your negative payback, but never know when or how it's going to come back. Let's say you stole something from someone, and you know that it was wrong, but you may think that you got away with it. Maybe for the moment you did, but there is no way you can avoid karma. One day you may lose your money when you least expect it and find yourself wondering why that happened to you. Because karma comes out of nowhere.

It just hits you, so be careful what you do, and of the bad energy that you put out in the world. "Karma is like a rubber band. You only stretch it so far before it comes back and smacks you in the face." So, beware.

Now, on the other hand, the same is true about dharma. You put out good and good comes back to you. The energy that you put out into the universe gets returned to you the same way you send it out. Dharma is practicing good that will bring you to serve your real purpose in life. "Seek your highest self. Discover your unique talents. Ask yourself how you are best suited to serve humanity. Using your unique talents and serving others brings unlimited bliss and abundance."- Deepak Chopra. So, every day you have to practice the law of dharma and watch how magically the universe will return it to you. But it all starts with your mind, so ask yourself if you are ready to reboot your mind and start a new beginning. "Unless you learn to face your own shadows, you will continue to see them in others, because the world outside of you is only a reflection of the world inside of you." I know this may be a big step and many may find it difficult. It may even seem farfetched because I've been there and done that.

At one point in time my life was a wreck. I had no life balance, which we cover in the next chapter. I was all over the place, my faith, and the light at the end of the tunnel just seemed so impossible to reach. I went broke, I was homeless, I had no car, and my license even got suspended. I was going through the ringer and couldn't seem to catch a break. It was like everything that could go wrong in my life was going wrong. I just couldn't understand why. I was well educated. I had my goals in order and knew what I wanted to do in life. I wasn't a bad person, but I wasn't considering where I went left. I wasn't looking at my environment. I wasn't looking at what I called my peace. I wasn't looking at the fact that I was playing victim and complaining. I wasn't looking at the energy that I was putting out into the universe. There were plenty of times I just wanted to break down and just give up on my life and my future. But it was that little gut feeling that kept reminding me that I could change. I could be a wonderful person and have happiness and peace in my life. I remembered that I was created to grow and evolve as a person. It was all a mental thing. Ugly thoughts will pop up in your head telling you to give up and telling you that it's too hard. But you better not dare give up. I'm am living proof that once you change your mind and environment then your life will unfold just as you predicated it to. So, no matter what, never give up and keep pushing forward until life stops fighting against you and starts fighting with you. "Magic happens when you do not give up, even though you want to. The universe always falls in love with a stubborn heart." And that's just what happened with me. I changed my whole mindset and that's when life started showing me what it had to offer if I displayed patience, faith, dharma, consistency, dedication, and a will to win in the game called life. I showed life that I am not a victim, but a survivor.

You have to be real with yourself. Everything starts with you. Just like that my life did a total 360 and so can yours. Don't worry about what you can't control or do; worry about what you can control, which is your mind. Changing your mindset and way of thinking will lead you to the next level of life and closer to your destination. Just like Tom Hanks said in the movie *Forest Gump*, "Life is like a box of chocolates. You never know what you're gonna get." But you damn sure can bargain for what you want in life. But first, you have to change your mindset. Get rid of toxic people and all of those ugly thoughts in your head. A good thing to do is every time you get a negative thought replace it with a positive thought. That's how you combat your mind until you can better get it under control and create your own remedy. I use this technique to this day, and it is very effective. Remember, there are people rooting for you that you have never met, so make it count. Now ask yourself, *who is really holding me back?* Nobody but yourself.

Level Up: Entrepreneur Spirit Blueprint

CHAPTER 7

LIFE BALANCE: THE CROSSOVER

"Balance is not something you find, it's something you create."

Now that you have removed the toxic waste from your mind and toxic people from your life, it is time that you form some type of life balance. This is the next step to get your life back on track. Before we jump into this chapter let me make something clear; no matter what you do in life, there must be balance for you to reach your highest potential and to be successful. So why not use these qualities to create your own empire? Why use these qualities to make someone else's dream come true? I want this book to bring out the inner entrepreneur that we all possess. Life balance is another key component for building an entrepreneurial foundation. Just as a house needs a solid secure piece of land before it can be built, the same applies to life balance. This is the first step to a new beginning and healthy foundation for entrepreneurship. If you don't have life balance your chances of being a successful entrepreneur are slim to none. Therefore, it is very important to have life balance before pursuing your goals and dreams "Life is about balance; too much and too little of anything is not good for you. The best way to balance life is setting your boundaries and learning to say ENOUGH."

I want to spend some time explaining why life balance is key. This is one of the common steps that many count out. Many people know how to change their mindset, but they don't know how to get reorganized after removing unwanted things from their life, which makes it hard to grow, adjust, and enjoy the process of making your dreams come true. There must be balance with everything you do. I am going to break down life balance, which includes family balance, career balance, health balance, and friend balance.

HEALTH BALANCE is the most important and valuable, because if you are not in good health, or at least trying to upkeep on your health, you will be no good to execute anything. Stress is a major killer and the growing point for many diseases, such as high blood pressure, cancer, mental illness, etc. Whatever you do, please have a plan to balance out your stress because stress will cloud your judgment. Try things like exercise, yoga, stress relief tea, etc. There are a host of things you can do to keep your stress levels down. you can even go on your search engine and type "ways to relieve stress." Good health also includes having "me time." Do things that you like to do. For example, my "me time" includes going to the spa and getting massages, manicures, and pedicures, or curling up in the bed and watching a good movie. Now, when you are getting your "me time," block out everything—work, family, and any issues. This is the time for you to regroup and reboot yourself to continue your day to day life with a fresh boost of energy, and if you can, I suggest turning off all phones, emails, electronics, etc. That way you can truly relax, have a clear head, and get the most out your "me time." Plan how often you need your "me time." I do mine twice monthly, every other Saturday, and that gives me the extra boost of energy to keep pushing forward. Afterwards, I just feel so rejuvenated like I can now take on the world. Incorporating this will relieve more stress than you think.

Also, make sure you are getting your regular checkups because the worst thing you can do is postpone a health issue that can eventually put you out of commission. Change your eating habits if necessary, such as incorporating more baked foods into your daily diet. Eat as many organic fruits and vegetables as possible. You will be surprised how a well-balanced meal plan can boost your mood, overall health, and energy. Try drinking fresh brewed teas as they have major health benefits and can help fight certain health issues. For instance, ginger tea is good for fighting cancer, controlling stress, helping the body absorb nutrients, protects against Alzheimer's disease, and helps a host of other issues. Chamomile tea is good for your skin, hair, and overall health. It boosts your immunity and has anti-aging properties because of the powerful antioxidants that it contains. Just like ginger tea, chamomile tea is soothing and relaxing and reduces stress. Incorporating some of these natural remedies can be a game changer for your health as well as your overall performance. Furthermore, make sure you incorporate a daily multivitamin as well as fish oil into your health regimen because whatever vitamins and minerals you lack from meals you can get in your vitamins. I take sea moss, a multivitamin, and vitamin C tablets every day. This will keep your immune system strong. When you have a strong immune system, you can combat illness better. Meal prepping is also another great regimen to adopt because it frees you up on time. And on those long work nights when you don't feel like cooking, you can pop one of your pre-cooked meals in the oven or microwave. I guarantee you that if you prep for the week, your life will be how much easier. I prep my breakfast, lunch, and dinner for the week, put them in containers, and freeze them.

Then as I need them pull them out. There's nothing like a healthy home-cooked meal that's within arm's reach. Now if you want to meal prep, I suggest doing it on Sundays, so you are ready and equipped for the week. I know some people say they don't have enough time to prepare meals or eat a balanced meal, but just remember, "those who think they have no time for healthy eating will sooner or later have to find time for illness." Please take care of your body. You only get one. In addition, make sure you are getting the proper sleep because lack of sleep can have unwanted side effects, like heart disease, heart attack, diabetes, and even aging your skin. So, make sure you are getting at least 6-8 hours of sleep daily. Remember, your health is your biggest asset. Protect and guard it. Make sure you take extra good care of yourself no matter what is going on in your life. "Health is like money, we never have a good idea of its value until we lose it." –Josh Billings

FAMILY BALANCE - What does family mean? "Family is one of life's greatest blessings, and a unit of people that love and support each other through good times and bad." It is important to spend time with those you love most, such as children, your significant other, siblings, parents, etc. Just as health balance is important so is family balance. You have to make sure that you don't neglect your family and loved ones, because you might look up one day and they will be gone. Cherish every moment you get to spend with your loved ones and always keep in mind to "never get so busy making a living or anything else that you forget to make a life, because there's no replacement for a family lost." A good idea is to have family night and date night if you have a partner. So, everyone has something to look forward to, and there is a balance between everything and everyone. It's a give and take kind of thing but in the end, everyone walks away happy, moving at the same pace. I have seen plenty of relationships and families break up because there was no family balance. There are seven days in a week, therefore, you get seven chances to balance. There's nothing like having a close-knit family by your side and coming home to them after a long day of work.

The number of things you are juggling will determine how much time daily or weekly you get to evenly divide and balance between them. Everyone will balance their life differently. There's no set way. Just long as you incorporate everything into your life. For example, someone who has no kids, but a significant other will balance their life differently versus a couple who has children, a single parent, or a single person with no partner or kids. To sum this up, you have to make the most out of your time. Once things get off track then that's when things can go left. Create a monthly calendar. Have scheduled meetings, workdays, family night/gatherings, and social time with friends, so that you can plan around that. If you have family balance everything else will fall into place. Planning a proper family balance is everything because this is one of the biggest obstacles that many face. It makes it so much harder to thrive and grow when frustration, stress, disappointment, and other issues arise due to feeling like you have to choose between family and other aspects of your life. This is avoidable. All you have to do is balance everything out. You want to always have a healthy family balance because that's where your peace is.

Family is important for several reasons. For one, family provides support and security. If you cannot turn to anyone else, you can definitely turn to your family for this. Family provides unconditional love, no matter what you are doing or going through, so it's only right that you cherish and appreciate your family. Secondly, family will protect you from external influences, such as peer pressure and bad decision making. Think about it, how many times were you thinking about doing something but wasn't sure, so you called one of your family members to provide you with honest advice and direction. Or you met someone new, whether a friend or business partner and you needed your family's insight. There is nothing like being able to turn to your family. Now I know not all families are always peaches and cream, but it is your family and at the end of the day and most family members will not steer you in the wrong direction. We all have some family members that we wish we could trade in, and I know not everyone is blessed with genuine family members, because that's the world we live in, but with most family members you should feel safe and secure with, and be able to count on, and turn to no matter what. If you cannot turn to them or something just does not feel right, then they are not your family, they are relatives. We just discussed toxic people, so you already know what you have to do. Just because two people have the same blood running through them that does not make them family. Family is who you can call your comfort zone and your safe house. In addition, if you have children, there's nothing like having your family help raise and support your children as they grow up, and also giving you a helping hand to free yourself up.

If you don't have a family, create one. You know how many good friends I have that I consider family? I have made my own sisters, cousins, aunts, and now I am even blessed with a mother-in-law. You don't have to have the same blood to be family. Loyalty makes you family. So, surround yourself with family who have your best interest at heart. Appreciate it and consider that your biggest blessing. Family help shape you into who you are as a person. Family is your backbone. Family is who you can trust, be honest with, and who helps brings out the best in you. Family gives you the boxing gloves to keep getting into the ring and keep fighting for what you believe in. When you have family by your side you will never feel alone as you tackle the world. So, ask yourself this question: who is your family? "Being a family means you are a part of something very wonderful. It means you will love and be loved for the rest of your life no matter what."

WORK LIFE BALANCE - Now that we've covered health and family balance, let's talk about what it means to have work life balance. First and foremost, when it comes to work life balance the first thing you must know is when to turn that switch off. You have to know when to detach yourself from your work and learn when to say enough. You cannot just work your life away. Remember, too much of anything is not good for you. So many people don't know when to step away from the workplace and leave work at work. I know for some it may be difficult, especially if you are an entrepreneur, because your job is never done and you may do a lot of work from home, but you have to know when to step away from work and hang that hat up. Why is it important to have work-life balance? Because it creates a wall that stops you from burning yourself out. I understand that some people are workaholics, but to consistently function that way can be draining and do more damage than help. Also, when you don't have work life balance you will find it hard to perform your best work because you are eating, sleeping, and pooping out work. Think about this! Have you ever tasted something for the first time, and it was so good, so you kept eating it until it didn't taste the same anymore? And after a while you turn your nose up every time you see it because you overdid it. Well, that's similar to not having work life balance. After a while you will get disgusted and less motivated if you keep working and incorporating your work life into everything you do, such as family and personal time. You will drive yourself crazy, your energy will go out the door, and doubts will start to sit in. You will lose that enthusiastic attitude and approach that you once had about your entrepreneur journey.

It is ok to leave work at work, and if you are an entrepreneur and work from home since you control all aspects of your company then set a work schedule for yourself and stick to it. Set how many hours a day you want to work. Even though you may go over your scheduled hours, especially in the beginning stages, try your best to stick to it as much as possible. And, if you are an employee, make sure that once you leave work you leave all your work problems at work. The purpose of this skill is to avoid letting your work life consume your overall life. "In between goals is a thing called life. That has to be lived and enjoyed." – Sid Caesar

In addition, this allows you to spend time doing things you like because when you have work life balance you are at your highest level of growth, whether you are an entrepreneur or an employee. "You can't do a job if your job is all you do."

FRIEND/SOCIAL BALANCE - Last but definitely not least, you must know when it is time to play and when it is not time to play. Outside of work, family, and managing your health, there is nothing like a healthy social balance. Whether your social life includes dating or just hanging around friends and associates, there must be a balance between it all. Sometimes you have to take a break and ley your inner kid out. There is nothing the matter with hanging out with some good friends with good energy to escape all the responsibilities that adulthood comes with. It is not easy being an adult. I remember when I was a kid, I used to say *I can't wait until I am grown up*. Now that I am grown, I say I wish I were still a kid! What was I thinking? Just make sure you don't get too caught up in having so much fun that you get distracted and thrown off track from what's really important. Go ahead and take a break. Catch up with some friends and have an outing for the day, such as a movie, lunch, or dinner, or even visit a nice lounge with some really good music. Friend/social balance should never feel pressured, overwhelming, or even make you feel like it is a priority. I mean it is important, but it shouldn't consume or impact your overall life. Good friends will understand that you have a life to maintain and responsibilities to keep up with. They will understand that it is not an all the time thing, just a gathering every so often. And furthermore, if you have friends who just want to hang out all the time then that means they have too much time on their hands, lack responsibilities, and that's not a good crowd that you want to hang around anyway. Your friend/social balance should be a reflection of you. Remember that old saying, "Birds of a feather flock together." You should always hang around people who are like minded and add value and positive energy to your life.

"Good friends are like stars. You don't always see them, but you know they're always there." Bonds cannot be broken, only promises. For instance, my best friend and I barely see each other, but that doesn't mean that our friendship is dying or fading away. She has goals that she is accomplishing and working on, and so do I. When we do meet up, we have so much fun. Since we barely get a chance to hang out, we have a ball and turn into big kids. When we finally see each other, it's nothing but love and laughter. We catch up with each other about life, what projects we are currently working on, we exchange advice, and talk about what we've been up to and why we were missing in action. We may go a few months without seeing each other. But we talk on the phone and text each other often. That's the kind of friendship you need; someone who is not going to make you feel bad because you are not hanging around them all the time because they understand each other's roles and lifestyles.

After defining what life balance is and ways to incorporate it into your daily life, here are a few signs that you may be lacking life balance. Firstly, does your body at times feel pain for no reason at all? Headaches, shoulder, or back pain? That's a sign that your body may be in constant strain and you may want to take a step back. That is your body warning you to slow down. Secondly, are you always feeling sleepy? That's your brain forcing you to slow down. Do you have a short stick of patience? Are you always on the verge of snapping and consistently feeling frustrated? That's a sign you are beginning to overwhelm yourself and don't know which direction to go because life is pulling you every direction but the right direction. Also, when was the last time you had a good laugh or just went out and enjoyed yourself and got to escape reality for a second? Do you find it hard to want to have fun and you are constantly shutting down? Well that's another sign that your body is getting tired of fighting the everyday daily activities and your body needs some TLC. Do you feel like your relationships with friends and family are going downhill and don't understand why? That's a sign of neglect.

Just as a flower needs water to grow or else

it will die, the same is true about a friendship balance. If you don't maintain it then it will eventually die. Do you find it difficult to keep your home and workspace organized and neat? Did you ever hear that if your house is a mess it's a reflection of your life? That's true! Are you all over the place when it comes to your priorities and can't distinguish between the most and least important things to tackle? That's because your brain is in overload and doesn't know what to do because you put too much on your plate without proper portions. If you can relate to any of these situations, then change is needed. Sit back for a minute and do some reflection on your life and make some rearrangements of the things that you placed on your plate because you will keep running into brick wall after brick wall and will never understand the cycle of why this keeps happening to you when all it takes is just a look in the mirror. It starts with you! If you want change, you have to be willing to leave old habits behind to make room for the new and beneficial habits. No matter what path you decide to take in life this is your starting point, so create it wisely and be as open as possible with yourself. The key to life balance is to realize "life balance is not better time management, but better boundary management"- Betsy Jacobson

So, how do you feel about your current position in life? How far away are you from organizing your life and having life balance? Do you have to make minor or major changes in your life? These are some of the things you need to think about now and fix them before you do anything thing else. Grab a pen and paper and write how you pictured your life to be on one side, and on the other side picture how your life currently is. Compare the two and make the necessary changes until your current life is parallel to your expectations and then you are well on your way.

Let's back track on everything that we covered thus far, to make sure we are on the same page because you can read all you want but if you are not grasping and retaining valuable information then it is pointless. I want you to get the most out of this book so it can bring out the best in you because I believe in you and I know you are capable of doing and becoming anything that you put your mind to. We are a few chapters away from you either entering the entrepreneur spirit or realizing this path is not for you. We are a few pages away from you discovering who you are as a person, what path you want to pursue, and the steps to reach your purpose in life. Are you still up for the challenge? Are you still willing to enter the entrepreneur spirit? Are you going to let a little extra work and dedication stop you? I didn't think so. You should have a clear understanding of the difference between an entrepreneur and the entrepreneur spirit. You should now have a clear understanding of your why behind wanting to be a true entrepreneur. You should have a clear understanding of the pros and cons of both being an employee and an entrepreneur. And even though entrepreneurship is a lot of hard work and risk, it is the most beneficial and most rewarding. You should understand that in order to have a new mindset you have to remove toxic things from your life, even if it means going separate ways from family and friends. You should have a clear understanding why life balance is so important and why it plays a major role in how far you will climb the ladder of success. Now the following chapters will cover even more tools and background skills needed to be a successful entrepreneur, so let's go you ready! I can't wait to see you enter the entrepreneur spirit.

Level Up: Entrepreneur Spirit Blueprint

CHAPTER 8

BACKGROUND AND SKILLS

"Hire character, train skill."

Just like with anything else you want to be successful in, you have to have the proper knowledge and experience to be an entrepreneur. If you want to be a successful entrepreneur and cut your risk in half, the first thing you must first realize is that knowledge is power. The more power you have the less risk you will accumulate. I cannot stress enough how important education is. "Education is the passport to the future, for tomorrow belongs to those who prepare for it today."- Malcolm X

No matter what, education is a flight of steps that you cannot cheat. Your success is going to make sure of that. Now I'm not saying that you must get a college degree, even though I strongly encourage obtaining a degree. There are many successful people who never stepped foot into a college classroom or who were college dropouts and are very successful and are even millionaires, such as Bill Gates, Oprah Winfrey, Steve Jobs, and Mark Zuckerberg. They chose to drop out to pursue their dreams full-time and didn't look back. They didn't just drop out of any college either. Some of them were attending Harvard University or Princeton University, which are the top colleges in the United States. What I am saying is that whether you choose to go to college or not, you must educate yourself some kind of way, whether it be local seminars, certifications, or self-help books, such as this one, which will give you a head start in the entrepreneur world. Make sure you are staying on top of your education and learn as much as possible. This is going to be your biggest defense against failure. "The educated differ from the uneducated as much as the living from the dead." – Aristotle

I do encourage anyone to obtain a college degree, even though it does not define your level of success. It can still help in many ways. Another reason why I'm all for college is because as an entrepreneur you can use the information as you're learning it, which makes it easier for you to retain the information because you are practicing it on a daily basis. You can also gain some long-term connections, as well as have a chance to join fraternities or sororities, which is always a plus. It is always a good idea to have a college degree under your belt because you never know when you may need to use it. Also, it makes it easier for you to view things from all angles of the business. For example, when you are ready to build and hire your team members, you will have knowledge in that area, making it easier for you to pick the perfect candidate because you have knowledge and you know what to look for in a possible employee and what to expect from them. But, again, I understand the college life is not for everyone. Just make sure you have a socket in which you can draw knowledge from. Education allows you to change the world. Isn't that what being an entrepreneur is all about—making changes and adding value? Nelson Mandela once said, "Education is the most powerful weapon which you can use to change the world." So, if you want to be an asset to the world you first must change the kind of knowledge you intake so you can output greatness. Also, if you want to be an entrepreneur you must know their makeup, such as their characteristics and skills. Below are some of the natural traits that most entrepreneurs have.

Characteristics of a True Entrepreneur

Entrepreneurs are very self-motivated and believe in the light at the end of the tunnel. Their focus and energy are what create a magical drive to keep fighting for what they want. Entrepreneurs are good at thinking outside the box and figuring out new ways to do things and break into the market. Entrepreneurs are very creative. Entrepreneurs can adapt and play any role in the chain of command for the most part and have basic knowledge of all the roles and responsibilities within the organization. They are very versatile. Entrepreneurs have great communication, finance, and management skills, and some basic knowledge of economics. I cannot stress this enough. Education is key! The more education you acquire the greater the reward and the lower your risk will be with basic business skills. Entrepreneurs are big risk takers. They know how to handle it and make sound decisions when the odds are against them. They know how to ride the ups and downs of the market in order to reap the rewards because of their risk tolerance. If there's a will there's a way and that's the theory that entrepreneurs live by. There is no such thing as impossible when it comes to a problem.

For example, look at the Covid-19 pandemic. It forced entrepreneurs to think outside the box and get their creative juices flowing to keep the cash flow coming in. They didn't just give up their business. They didn't complain and lose hope even though it was frustrating and lots of entrepreneurs lost huge profits due to this world crisis. Instead, true entrepreneurs just adjusted to the change and that's the most important thing when it comes to being an entrepreneur; being able to adjust. They didn't just throw their business away. They coped with the change and readjusted the way they do business and interact with customers. For instance, the restaurant business took a hit big time and was forced to shut down. But what did business owners do? They switched to carry-out only and utilized services such as Door Dash and Uber Eats. Sure, businesses have slowed down due to the pandemic, but it didn't stop a true entrepreneur.

Let's back track for a minute and play devil's advocate. Now, remember in the early chapters when I was explaining the difference between being an employee versus an entrepreneur? Well, let's take a look at the Covid-19 pandemic and how millions of people lost their jobs, struggled through the pandemic, are unsure what the future holds, and/or will have no job to return to. Millions of people have had to apply for unemployment. This is what I'm referring to when I talk about bout not putting all your eggs in one basket. This highlights the importance of always having a side hustle or multiple strands of income, so that when one income slows down you can turn to another income to get you by. Also, yes, business owners suffered too and some are facing bankruptcy, but guess what? They can get certain incentives for simply being a small business owner. For example, workers got a one-time stimulus check for about $1,200 while businesses got grants and loans to help pay their payroll, overhead expenses, etc. and help keep their businesses from shutting down. We are living in uncertain times and you cannot depend on a company to keep you safe. You have to prepare yourself for anything that could happen that would jeopardize your livelihood. And, not to mention when times got hard for businesses lots of them sold some of their stock to help them survive. You see the difference, right? Small businesses will always be protected more than the average worker will. I'm not saying workers are not covered. But some are not. Jobs like waitress, bartender, etc. don't really come with benefits and a lot of people who have these types of jobs get paid under the table, don't file taxes, and/or don't pay taxes, so when things hit the fan then they lose out for the most part with barely any coverage. So, when securing a job know your benefits and how you will be covered and protected as far as job security.

I say all this to say that although entrepreneurs go through all the obstacles looking struggle and failure in the face, they how to keep pushing forward while weathering any storm. Entrepreneurs are very good visionaries. As I mentioned in the beginning chapter, they can see the big picture when it may be blurry to others. They understand that others may not get their vision until it actually becomes reality, so they must be big on self-motivation because many will doubt and second guess their plan and/or business ventures. Entrepreneurs are good at getting anything executed as long as the rewards are greater than the risks, and they are very good at adapting to change. This is one of their greatest traits. They create innovational ways to approach a new or existing market because of their open minds. Covid-19 forced the world to turn more virtual and online, opening many doors for new ways of doing business, creating new markets for new niches and new businesses to be born. Covid-19 forced people to do their own thing and start their own businesses to bring in money since they may have been laid off. I have seen people making custom masks and selling them, driving for Uber Eats, etc.

Entrepreneurs know the grass will not always be greener on the other side but that will not affect their confidence level one bit. They believe in starting the venture and bulletproofing the plan then allowing others to follow, lead, and run the company as planned. They set the tone and create the blueprint. Entrepreneurs are great self-starters. Entrepreneurs are very competitive at times. They feel like they have to hit a homerun at the business venture they created. They have so much on the line and have made so many sacrifices, so they believe their next move must be their best move. All entrepreneurs do is eat, sleep, and poop their business. The only thing on their mind is work, work, and more work. That's why a life balance is essential for an entrepreneur to have, or at least try to have.

Once they set a certain expectation, they will meet it, no matter what. Entrepreneurs have many sleepless nights and will literally work from sunup to sundown, because once they slack then the plan could be postponed and delayed. Entrepreneurs hate procrastination because the longer it takes to meet a goal the longer they must delay the project. It is like your pace determines your place in the race, and entrepreneurs don't like to settle for anything less than first place, especially when they have so much invested into their business venture. Entrepreneurs are very passionate about what they are doing. They take it seriously and follow their passion and then the money follow afterwards. That's why they don't care about making the money in the beginning; they know the money will come eventually. Entrepreneurs are very connected and emotional about their business. It is similar to carrying an infant in the womb. You nourish, feed, and do all the right things so when the infant is born it is a healthy bundle of joy. There's no better feeling. You put in all that hard work and can't wait to see what you created; it's an amazing feeling because it belongs to you. It is a part of you and, most importantly, your company is a reflection of you. You care for you child out of passion, you love your child out of passion, you chose to be a parent out of passion. You don't do any of those things for money, you do them for passion. The same goes for your company. Don't do it for the money. Do it because it is your passion because it you do it for the money you will never enjoy the process of being a true entrepreneur. I started many companies because the money seemed so enticing, which frustrated and stressed me out even more. I remember when I went to cosmetology school, I did it because of the income stream it could create and not because it was my passion. I was really good at doing hair and made a lot of money but I wasn't happy doing it, and every day I woke up I had to talk myself into doing hair until eventually I got tired of making excuses for why I was doing it. So, I just let that business venture go. I wanted to enjoy what I was doing. I wanted to be happy and amazed at my work. In the chapter I will discuss finding your passion and turning it into a revenue fountain. Now that you have taken a look into the entrepreneurial mind and entrepreneurial skills you should have a better understanding of how entrepreneurs function. Are you ready to transition and adjust to those habits? If so, I outlined some ways to adopt entrepreneurial skills.

How to Build Entrepreneurial Skills

Not everyone is a natural born entrepreneur, but the good part is that you can learn how to become an entrepreneur. Here are some of the things that you can incorporate into your life to build solid entrepreneurial skills.

Take a Different Path - Create your own niche. Create a market that didn't exist before or expand an existing market. Entrepreneurs are the voice of the people. They know what society wants, and they do what it takes to satisfy that market. Their job is to make the impossible possible and help non-believers become believers.

Start a Business - Become your own boss now that you have the entrepreneur mindset. You have your why behind wanting to start a business and becoming your own boss. Now is the time. Just remember the word "boss" is a big title and comes with lots of responsibility. You control many people's livelihood, so you have to be ready because a lot of people will be depending on you to make the company a success. Besides, you will be creating new jobs for the public, which can be a scary thing because you have to make sure the business is doing well enough to cover every cost possible, and even the unexpected costs that may come with running your own business. People will be depending on you to feed their family by adding income to their bank in exchange for their labor. You have to be ready to step into this field and a true entrepreneur. It's either all the way or not at all. When entrepreneurs step out, they are ready and well equipped for the business world. This book will give you a jump start and help you avoid a lot of pitfalls. You just have to be willing to start. And don't think you have to be great to start. No, you just have to start to be great.

Stick with the Challenges - Entrepreneurs understand that they have to stick with the good, bad, and ugly. They don't just run away the first time they see an obstacle. Instead, they figure out a way to knock that obstacle down. They are fearless. Actually, they get a rush when obstacles come their way because, again, entrepreneurs are problem solvers, and the more obstacles they face the sharper they will be in their industry, so they welcome obstacles wholeheartedly.

Manage your Assets - Balance your personal and business assets, and also set aside for rainy days because they will happen. An entrepreneur will fail countless times before they finally get their big break. So, until then, even when the money is coming in and you think that things are going smooth, as a rule of thumb, always live below your means. This is discussed in a later chapter as well. When you do that you will keep striving and you will never get comfortable. the plan is to be uncomfortable until you have no choice but to be comfortable once you have steady flowing income and wealth. The worst thing you can do is try to keep up with the Joneses when starting a new business, because most businesses fail within the first five years. So again, no matter what, live below your means. You always have to have that little cushion to protect you for unexpected forecasts that will arise. If you follow and plan properly you can avoid major pitfalls.

Volunteer to Lead - Practice becoming a leader, even if you are not getting paid. Do this to gain experience, network and be a productive member in society. Start doing fundraisers or even volunteer to do jobs that will help you gain the knowledge and experience needed for you to become a successful entrepreneur, and to run your empire efficiently and effectively. You have to be willing to be a sponge and absorb as much knowledge as possible and be around like-minded people. It's always good to learn from some else's mistakes, if possible. And remember what we discussed: knowledge is power! The more knowledge you have, the more powerful your company will be, and the chances for your company to be successful will be great. Never stop learning. Keep up with the trends and the latest. Furthermore, volunteering looks good for your resume and credentials to show that you care about your community and the people in it.

Practice Communication Skills - Take some public speaking classes. How can you get anyone to believe in your passion if you don't know how to convey the message right? This is a key skill because your communication skills will help you gain an audience. I encourage you to take some type of public speaking or communication classes. Another alternative is to volunteer to speak at local gatherings, which will give you plenty of practice and help you overcome your fears for when you have to speak to a large crowd.

Find a Mentor - It is critical to find a mentor who is already successful in your chosen industry. If you don't do anything else, please get a mentor. There is nothing smarter than learning from someone who has already mastered the industry that you are about to step into. You can learn the past and current trends from them so you can better predict the future trends. In order to have a successful business you have to know the evolution of that industry, and what better way to learn than from the giants of that industry?

Meet Other Entrepreneurs – Remember, your network is your net worth. Get out and go to local events. Support other entrepreneurs along they journey. When they have events, go to them. That's an opportunity to partner up with them and also to meet new people that can be an asset to your business venture. Out of sight, out of mind. If you are not in the mix attending events how are you going to grow your brand and meet new people? Even if your company is still in the early stages, get involved with as many events as possible. You never know who you might connect with that can help your business grow even faster, or that can land you the opportunity that you have been waiting forever for. Don't be scared to let people know you are new to the entrepreneur world. Even if you are still in the baby stages, you will be surprised by the help that will come your way. "Entrepreneurs are like sharks. They die when they stop moving forward." By this point I'm sure you are ready to keep moving forward. If not, what's stopping you?

CHAPTER 9

PATIENCE

"To lose patience is to lose the battle."

Sometimes the fastest way isn't always the best way. Sometimes the best things in life take a while."- Emily Beth. With that being said, you never want to rush greatness. You could miss you moment just because you could not wait for things to unfold as you wanted to. This is where you have to trust yourself and trust the process. Sometimes there is a better plan for you, and you may not see it because you are rushing what you have set forth. Patience can save you from unforeseen pain and pitfalls. Patience can bring opportunities your way but the only way you will know is if you have patience. Having patience also means that you don't lose your cool. No matter what the situation is around you, let it pass its course. Nothing last forever; whatever might be holding you back or is in your way soon will pass if you just stick around to see. Some people so quick to give up or take a different route when all they had to do was have a little patience. Patience can make or break you and time reveals all things, whether good or bad. You ever hear someone say you're moving too fast? I know I did. It was hard for me to practice patience at first. I wanted everything to happen right then and there, and if it didn't, then I would get frustrated, panic, and my anxiety would kick in. I caused my own illness when all I had to do was let things flow how they were going to flow. It took me years to learn this, especially being an entrepreneur, because there was so much that I wanted to accomplish, and I felt like I was on the clock. It hurt me more than it helped me. For one, it caused me to jump around between different projects because I didn't have the patience to watch one project blossom at a time. In my head I would think a project was a failure and move on to the next project when all I had to do was have patience.

I remember as a young adult I wanted to start a doggy clothing line. I drew my designs, took all the right steps, found a seamstress and everything. I went the whole nine yards, but it seemed like everything was taking too long. then I figured maybe it was not a good idea. And this was way before animal clothing became popular. Instead of me doing my proper research, and slow stepping my venture I just gave up on it and look how big the market for animal clothing is now. If only I would have been patient, I would have got my piece of the pie, too. But I didn't so my whole idea went down the drain and became someone else's.

Now let's really study patience. Take love, for instance. You take your time to build a relationship with your possible mate. You take your time to get to know everything about your partner. You take your time to see if you and your partner are a good match. You take your time to love one another and what happens down the road after you build a bond and know the good and bad about each other? Marriage, right? It took hard work and patience to get to that point. That's how you have to pursue everything in life. If you want it bad enough then it should be worth the wait. Anything that is worth having is worth the wait. So, if you want success bad enough it is worth the wait. If you want to change something, then it is worth the wait. Don't be in a rush to do anything in life or everything you ever wanted will walk right past you. You know what's so special about patience? Remember when I said time reveals all things? It is really patience that reveals all things. Use patience as a weapon. It is vital in all situations in life and even more vital as you become an entrepreneur. See, to truly endure or grasp the entrepreneur spirit with anything you do in life, patience is necessary because there may be times when you question your journey or road to becoming an entrepreneur, or don't fully grasp the impact. There are moments in life where you'll create a rite of passage for the next generation of young entrepreneurs. Patience is what relaxes your mind along your journey, stops you from second guessing your desire, and allows you to continue driving yourself forward towards success and forward towards becoming an entrepreneur. Free your mind from negative thoughts, which create doubt in your ability and automatically trigger your brain into a quitter's mind state. Patience allows you to abandon those thoughts and resign from negative actions and become more proactive by enjoying the journey and process of becoming an entrepreneur! Allow your brain to relax and breathe. A full demonstration of patience is key in any battle tested situation. The first step to patience is steeliness. Do nothing, calm yourself from being overwhelmed, take a step outside your body, and trust your higher power and your intuition to guide your inner being. This will help you to make the best decision mentally, physically, and emotionally. The best way to master patience is to compartmentalize your thoughts. Break them down into three sections: good, great, and excellent.

Good is a standard that entrepreneurs should avoid because good won't make it in today's society of young entrepreneurs. There is always someone younger and hungrier waiting to win and operate inside your field of work who's pushing for greater! Good is an excuse tricking your mind into thinking your job is complete.

Great is a standard that's considerable, remarkable, impressive. Deep down within yourself, you as an entrepreneur knows it's just ordinary work. As an entrepreneur you know your strengths and weaknesses, and great isn't good enough!

Excellence shows in your work. It shows your patience. It shows your ability to compartmentalize, and your passion and commitment to your craft. It shows your militant mind of patience that your entrepreneurial work deserves its highest honor of excellence. Excellence comes from steeliness, a sense of calmness at its purest form of patience. Also, don't allow patience to compartmentalize your mind so much to the point that it become complacency. Compose your thoughts with steeliness and allow your entrepreneur spirit to roam freely. A creative mind is a powerful tool, your most valuable tool, but this amazing tool only functions properly by using extraordinary measures of patience and fully trusting your entrepreneur spirit. So now that we have that understood, next time you're tempted to lose your patience, think about what section you are in. Do you want to be good, great, or excellent in your journey of entrepreneurship? "Patience, persistence, and perspiration make an unbeatable combination for success." – Napoleon Hill

Now we are about to jump into part two of the book, which contains all the secret weapons that will assist you in climbing the mountain of success. So, brace yourself because you are now under the entrepreneur spirit, and you're about to find out why it is deeper than you think!

Level Up: Entrepreneur Spirit Blueprint

CHAPTER 10

LUCKY OR NOT?

"Luck always seems to be against the man who depends on it."

It's not called luck! This is where a lot of people get it twisted. Nothing is ever by luck. It is simply about opening up your third eye, also known as your sixth sense, to have the ability to trust the process. A lot of people don't know what kind of energy to put out into the universe because they have a misconception. The third eye gives you the abilities to achieve anything. It's like magic but good magic. The only way you can open your third eye is if you detach yourself from your environment/surroundings. You have to be ready for isolation so you will be able to get in tune with the universe. That's why you had to go through the detox stage in order for this to work. Your third eye is "your ability to see what might be", in other words, to see potential. Your third eye is like a bonus sense. Just like you have five senses, which are smell, sight, touch, taste, and sound, this is your sixth sense. People often don't know how to activate it, which is why they don't know how to be successful. That's why they confuse luck with the sixth sense/third eye, which is the last but key piece to the puzzle. That's when you achieve true success, and the greatest success, because you are at your highest energy level, your highest awareness level. You are at a point where you are able to draw the universe and what you want towards you. Anybody can open their third eye. That's the blessing of it. If you know what a hunch feels like, then you have the power to open your third eye. Your third eye is your ability to use your hunch, intuition, or gut feeling at the highest level. That's why the key to life is to start with yourself. You have to master self-greatness and self-belief. That's how you add greatness to the world, and that is when you then become a legend.

Have you ever had a bad feeling about something, and it just wasn't sitting well with you? You just knew something was wrong, so you followed your gut and later down the line you found out that your gut feeling was right. Here is something else to think about to show you that your sixth sense/third eye is real! Have you ever walked in a room and the energy was weird? That was your third eye picking up on that. Do you think you getting that feeling for nothing? No, that's your third eye trying to connect and get you to pay attention. Or have you ever been sad and put some music on and just like that your energy was different and your mood changed to you feeling better and not even worried about what bothered you in the first place? That's your third eye trying to get you to pay attention and control it. Your third eye makes all your other senses reach their highest point to make you razor sharp when making decisions. That's why it's important to protect your energy. Your surroundings and environment can hinder your third eye. Let's take misery for example. Have you ever been around someone and their mood was off, meaning they were moody, and you were in the happiest mood? What happened? Your mood started to change, and their energy started to attach to you. That's your third eye working but you just didn't know how to control it. That's why isolation is another important factor in protecting your third eye. "The isolated family member is usually the one who becomes awake." - Jim Carrey

That's why people who have opened their third eye meditate. They are learning how to control their mind to do what they want it to do verses their mind controlling them with all kinds of thoughts from their environment instead of the universe. Where do you think fear comes from? That's your mind telling you that it is controlling you, and you're not controlling it. Your mind gets you to believe all kinds of things that probably don't even exist. That is your mind playing tricks on you. And fear is the number one mind game that gets played on people. Why do you think fear is the number one paralyzer? Because your mind knows you are not strong enough to control it mentally, and fear will keep controlling your mind until it destroys you. Once you overcome fear and become fearless you have already beaten the odds and there is nothing mentally holding you back. "Too many of us are not living our dreams because we are living our fears."- Les Brown

Do you know that's what really stops people from reaching their full potential? They fear they are not good enough, and truthfully, that's why many people play it safe and get a stable job. Fear tells them they will never be an entrepreneur. I mean honestly, who wouldn't want to be their own boss and have their own establishment? Who wouldn't want to make their dreams come true if they had the opportunity to do so? As kids we all had these big, extraordinary dreams, and what happened? As we got older fear started creeping into our minds more and more until it had total control over our minds. Unfortunately, some survive fear, and some don't. That's why many people believe they are not strong or smart enough. They fear what others think, they fear what the outcome will be, they fear that they will never make it to the top, they fear that they are not ready, they fear that they will fail.

"Never let fear decide your future." Many people will never make it to the top because they let fear tear their courage and self-esteem down. Some people will be in an abusive relationship with themselves and fear. Don't ever be a victim of fear but show victory with courage. The only way you can overcome fear is to face your fears, control your mind, and open up your six sense. This will destroy fear every time. I promise it will. I found this cool acronym for fear on the internet that helped carry me along my journey. So, when fear starts to make its way in your mind remember fear is "False Evidence Appearing Real." I hope this can be of some use to you as well. Each level of your life demands a new version of yourself, which is called growth, and you become more and more fearless to have the abilities to open your natural God-given gifts. You cannot enter the entrepreneur spirit unless you reinvent yourself to go to the next level of your life. To have your third eye is to be aware. People call it luck because they don't know how to control their third eye/sixth sense to achieve what they want in life.

When all it is the capability to use your third eye fearlessly with opportunity to help you plot, plan, and execute. That's how you get your foot in the door. Stay ready and you never have to worry about getting ready. It's all about when opportunity meets preparation. Then you create your own luck. That's something you have to do, and many don't know how to do it. That's why when they see someone blossoming the first thing people say is "they are lucky." No, they prepared themselves to meet their opportunity, which changed their future forever. The key is your mind, effort, and hard work; you will have everything you ever wanted in life. That's why being an entrepreneur is a blessing to some and a curse to others because of the lack of knowledge. Now I'm not saying once you unlock and change your mindset and open your third eye or sixth sense then everything is going to come flowing in. I'm not about to sell you a fairy tale. I'm saying it just makes it easier for you to achieve success, to attract and focus on what you want. It makes it easier when you reach obstacles to challenge yourself to overcome it. It makes it easier to know that one day your hard work will pay off and the world will see the weight you carried on your shoulders. It makes it easier for you to appreciate life, even the small things, and to realize how blessed you are to use your mind to achieve your dreams. It makes it easier to know that you are the only one who controls your destiny in life. It makes it easier to know that every drop of blood, sweat, and tears that you shed will make you a legend and change many lives. It makes it easier to accept that you are a hero and you earned that title because many people will never be able to unlock the magic that's in their mind. The saying is so true; "a mind is a terrible thing to waste." Why do you think people fear losing their mind? Because they understand their mind is the most powerful thing they own. So, if you want to really be successful, be successful all the way around the board. In order to be successful, you must first know success is not what you have materialistically or your title. It's about where your mind is. Get in tune now. It is never too late. It's better to start late than to never start at all.

Now, that you know don't ever say someone is lucky or that you wish that you were lucky like them. We all have the same 24 hours to do the same thing. It is up to you how you utilize your time and mind. Gain all the knowledge possible and open your third eye. You will achieve whatever you want in life. You have to let the universe know what you want because if you don't then the universe won't give it to you. "Magic happens when you do not give up, even though you want to. The universe always falls in love with a stubborn heart." It is all a test and those who pass get what they want out the universe. Also, you have to learn how to protect your potential by opening up your third eye, because that's why those self-doubts start creeping into your head. You hear people talk about how their energy is low or drained. Can you imagine if you could reverse that and your energy now allowed you to see how your motions, actions, and judgment will fit right into place to have the ability to see your future dreams turned into reality? It's all in the mind. As you can see, greatness starts within the mind and is the most powerful tool, so you have to be gentle and handle it with care. Change your mind and change your life forever. The entrepreneur spirt is only a blessing if you expand your mind and a curse once you don't test your inner abilities. Your curse begins with the question mark after a bunch of doubtful, regretful questions like *what if I would have...?* Now that we've discussed that, who's ready to eat some humble pie?

CHAPTER 11

BE HUMBLE OR CRUMBLE

"If you are humble nothing will touch you, neither praise nor disgrace, because you know what you are."

– Mother Teresa

The best beginnings are humble beginnings. Never brag or feel like you are better than the next person because we all go through the same things in life, just in different ways for different reasons. Do you know that by bragging you are setting yourself up for failure? In life you're never supposed to kick someone when they are down because that same person you kicked or feel like is below you, you may one day need. How would you feel if someone looked down on you because you didn't have what they had, or because you weren't as smart as them? Pretty bad I'm sure. You're always supposed to put yourself in the other person's shoes. Just remember, never judge a person's current situation because you never know what path or journey they may take in life. Furthermore, you never know what they went through in life. Being humble takes practice because I have heard many people say *I can't wait to get rich*, or *I can't wait until this plan goes through...I'm going to shit on this person* or *I'm going to show the world this, that, and the third*. That's not wise because the faster you get it the faster you can lose it, and what goes up must come down. That's a hell of a feeling because on your way coming back down you see everyone that you turned your nose up at once upon a time. Be careful because you never know when your life will go left.

Your title or status should never define you as a person. You should be the same way whether you are broke or rich, whether you have all the knowledge in the world or no knowledge at all. It is never attractive to be big headed. Nothing should change how you are as a person. If you don't humble yourself life will humble you for sure if you don't know how to do it. He who can be humble and have the world in is hands is the true strong one, and he who feels powerful because of what he possesses is weak. Now I'm not saying that you can't be confident and celebrate your achievements but never think that because you accomplished what others couldn't you are better than them. That is the wrong mindset to have and definitely not a trait of a true entrepreneur. Don't worry, you don't have to brag. Let others do it for you. Let your success speak for itself; everything you do doesn't need to be seen or heard. That is a complete turn off and can rub people the rub way. No matter how successful you are, no matter how big your house is, no matter how fancy your car is, no matter how much money you've got in the bank, stay humble. Steven M. R. Covey said "a humble person is more concerned about what is right than about being right, about acting on good ideas than having good ideas, about embracing new truth than defending outdated positions, about building the team than exalting self, about recognizing contribution, than being recognized for making it."

Being humble is cooler than being famous, so if you think being famous is amazing can you imagine what being humble feels like? Your grave will not look any different than the next person's grave. The only difference is the tombstone, but we are all going six feet under one day so try to be the best person that you can be. Instead of boasting about how your life has changed, help others change their lives. I have been around some real arrogant people, and it almost made me sick to see how a title can change a person. I always remove myself from the presence of those kinds of people because they are poison. There's Nothing like being around a down to earth person who has it all but acts as if they don't have a thing. That's the kind of person you want to be around. Never be around non-humble people because if they can treat others like crap when they have nothing how do you think they would treat you if you had nothing? Pay attention to people and see how they sit and act with people who are not as fortunate, and that will tell you a lot about their character.

Have you ever known or been around someone who was successful or had a bunch of money and their attitude sucked? They felt like the world owed them something. Then, you don't see them for a while and you happen to run into them, and they are doing bad, and you wonder what happened to them. Now, they are a totally different person. They are calmer and their whole demeaner switched up. That's because life humbled them, and I bet you if they get a second chance at success they will be humble because they now know what it feels like to be looked down on and have it all one minute and lose it the next minute. Sometimes God and the universe test you and will give it all to you just to see how you will react to it, then take it all away because you didn't deserve to have it. You didn't appreciate it and you didn't pass the blessings down, so life sat you right back down at the drawing board and said "now let's start over and try this humble thing again."

Another thing is that you don't ever want to get revenge to the point that it makes you no longer humble. I know in my personal experiences I have done and said things, especially to those who have hurt me or told me I wasn't going to be successful or make it. The first thing I said was *I can't wait to make it...I'm going to make them pay for all the mean things they said to me. I'm going to stunt on them as soon as I'm rich, and when I make it nobody better ask me for anything!* I'm blessed to not have adopted that mindset because my blessings would have gone out the door.

"You can't fight evil with evil. The only way to drive out darkness is thru light." So shine bright even when others are stuck in the dark, and never give someone so much power that you want to be successful just to stunt or prove a point to somebody, because that's still giving them control over you. Remember the silent goodbyes are the most powerful goodbyes. Out of sight, out of mind. So, whatever you do in life make sure it is always for the greater good because you are trying to be an entrepreneur, and true entrepreneurs add value to the universe, not take it away. Don't ever fall victim to pride because that is the opposite of being humble, and we all know pride gets you nowhere in life. Please don't place unnecessary curses upon yourself. You will have enough battles to fight. Don't add more battles than there needs to be. Also, be careful who you look up to because you should never be impressed by money, followers, degrees, and titles. Be impressed by kindness, integrity, humility, and generosity. Never forget where you came from because you never know when you may have to revisit. Where arrogant and boastful people go wrong is, they don't realize that their life is not a competition, and that's what humble people have mastered and understand. The universe responds well to humility because that shows you have the strength to place yourself at the same level as others and not above others, which ultimately gives you the highest level of self-control, and isn't that what entrepreneurship is about? Having self-control to make wise decisions? If you don't have any humble juice you better get some quick. That's the only way you will stay hydrated along your journey. I know this is an old saying, but it is very valuable: "treat others how you would want them to treat you." I think that is the best feeling, being successful and going back in the forest to rescue people and walk through the woods again and again to save more and more lives. People will never forget how you impacted their life, whether good or bad. Do the right thing and whenever you enter someone's life leave a positive impact.

Now, with that being said, how will being humble benefit you as an upcoming entrepreneur? Modesty is a trait that distinguishes one's character. Character is everything for a new entrepreneur. It tells a lot about who you're doing business with, so character goes along way. Being humble along your journey allow those inside your work field to know and understand that you're grateful for the opportunity. Humble is also a state of mind, and it takes self-confidence. Staying humble is a mental mind game you want to play with the opposition. The opposition may mistake your confidence and humbleness as a threat, a possible source of danger. Because in the business world you have to keep your poker face on but play chess at all times. We will get into that more in a later chapter when we talk about the wolves of the business world. Anyway, keep your head down and focus on working harder than everyone else. Allow being humble to drive and motivate you further as an entrepreneur. Being humble is gasoline for an already burning fire within you. Allow your character to blaze your trail to success! Warriors are humble, fear is a sure sign of chaos, which the opposition will show from being in your humble presence. Being humble allows you to shine and expose the wolves in sheep's clothing effortlessly. Your entrepreneur spirit will allow you to humble yourself in the work field. An entrepreneur understands patience and timing, and understands waiting on their moment can become taxing, because of young entrepreneurs' attention span. Everything is weird for right now, because we live in a microwave generation and want everything "hot and ready" at that very moment in time.

Being humble is a lost art. It requires patience, trust, and the self-awareness of knowing each star shines differently. Allow being humble to position your entrepreneurial star in a different direction to the highest point among titans. Being humble allows you to fly under the radar and become that industry titan amongst other well-respected giants. Being humble means having manners. Never allow someone to mistake those mannerisms of being humble for not being hungry. Being humble is training your mind and body. The entrepreneur spirit is your goal, so stay humble and ready. Your moment is around the nearest corner.

I love the struggle because the struggle will humble you before you reach success. "Rock bottom has built more her's than privilege." Your ultimate goal of being humble should be to "climb the mountain so you can see the world, not so the world can see you." Always starve your ego and feed your life by this motto and you will be on the road to having a wealthy mind and life.

CHAPTER 12

BUDGETING 101

"Be aware of little expenses. A small leak will sink a great ship."

Not only is having the right mindset important to be a successful entrepreneur, but you must also have the right tools to be able to execute your goals once you're ready to begin your journey. As an entrepreneur it is important that you have a cushion for rainy days, because when you first start your journey the path is never easy, and your money will fluctuate. You will never have a set income flowing in right away and, depending on your path, you may not see any profits for a few years. Always live below your means, even if money is flowing in. Don't think it's going to be steady. Prepare yourself for little potholes along the way, and the best way to do that is have a six-month survival plan. "When disaster strikes, the time to prepare has passed."- Steven Cyros

You're always supposed to pray for the best, but prepare for the worst no matter what, because you never know what future problems may arise. So how do you prepare for your six-month survival plan? All you have to do is add up all your monthly expenses and once you have that magic number multiply it by six and that's what you should have tucked away for any rainy days. The key is not to accumulate unnecessary debt, meaning taking on expenses that could be avoided. You have to live like you are broke even when you're not until your business takes off like you expect it to, and your company is keeping a steady cash flow every month. Until then, don't go buying a bunch of fancy clothes. It's okay to treat yourself once in a while, but what I am really talking about is don't have 50 million credit cards. If you can avoid financing a vehicle, do it because not only will you have to make your monthly payments, which can be pretty steep depending on how much money you put down, but also you have to consider your credit score rating. And you still have to pay car insurance, which can go from $150 up depending on your age, your driving record, and a couple of other factors. So alone that bill could be about $700-$1,000 monthly, not to mention the gas that you will be putting in the car. That's why the key is to avoid as many expenses as possible. You don't want to lose everything when it gets a little rough or tight.

Also, the less expenses you have the more you can save, and the more you can prepare and overcome any financial obstacles that may come your way. Basically, the only expenses you should have are your needs, not your wants. Your wants will come when your business is thriving. Until then, prepare yourself as best as you can for rainy days because trust me, they are coming. Another thing you don't want is to have so many expenses that if a problem arises you can't cover it and it ruin your credit because credit is better than money. Let's say your business is not growing how you expected it to. The money is not flowing in, and you have a mortgage, a car payment, credit cards etc. How are you going to cover those expenses? You risk getting your car repossessed, losing your house, and having charge offs for your credit cards. All this could damage your credit score badly, making it hard for you to get future lines of credit, loans, etc., and loans are critical when being an entrepreneur. Somewhere down the line you will need financial help, especially when it's time to expand your company. To avoid all that don't ever put yourself in that situation because it is avoidable. Don't worry about fancy cars, homes, or material things. Your focus should be on growing your business and building your cushion; that other stuff will come later down the line. Never try to keep up with the Joneses. Focus solely on your lane. You want to play it as safe as possible because being an entrepreneur is risky enough. And, if you do have any credit cards make sure it's only a few. If you have to use your credit cards, make sure you don't spend more than 35% of whatever your credit limit is. Doing this will boost your credit score up and have a positive impact on your credit report, making it easier when requesting more lines of credit on your existing credit card. For example, let's say your credit limit is $500…35% percent of that would be $175, meaning that's all you can spend from your $500 credit limit and you should not use the reminding balance. If you keep this pattern up for about six months straight, then you can request more credit. Now that doesn't mean that when you get more credit you should spend it. Keep doing the same thing and before you know it you will have more than enough credit for rainy days, investments, whatever you need to help along your journey.

In addition, make sure you always pay your credit card payments on time and pay a little extra if you can. That's always a plus and looks good to lenders. One thing you can do to make sure you don't forget it is you can enroll in automatic payments, which is always a plus. This is the method I use with my payments. And, not only that, when you enroll in autopay most creditors will give you extra perks for enrolling, so make sure you check with your creditor. You don't want to ever max out your credit cards because they will come in handy when you need them most. Look at credit cards as an extra savings account that you personally yourself didn't invest in. Don't ever let anyone use your name or credit because it will fall on you in the end. You will be responsible for that debt, not them, even if they did accumulate it. Hold on to your credit and guard it because you will need it somewhere down the line. Credit is better than money. Your credit score determines what type of person you are, meaning how responsible and reliable you are when it comes to paying back your debt. The goal should always be to Live below your means, build your credit, and save for rainy days while perusing your dreams. This will ensure less potholes along that area of your journey. You never know when you will need that extra cushion for your business for unexpected problems that will arise, so always be smart, play it safe, and never give yourself enough rope to hang yourself.

Also, you never want to put all your eggs in one basket. Ask yourself this question: what is your backup plan? Meaning if you do have to tap into your six-month survival money what will you do once that money runs out and until your company can recuperate? What do you plan on doing to keep yourself afloat to put that money back into your account? This is where you can pull tricks from out of your sleeve meaning this is where all those trades that you have under your belt will come in handy. That's why I said it's important for you to never stop learning and get as much under your belt as possible. They will come in handy when those rainy days start to surface and you may have to jump back into the work force to get back on track or put your hustler hat on to accumulate some extra cash until the storm passes. For instance, I have a finance background, a real estate background, and am a licensed cosmetologist and mixologist. I have entrepreneurship certifications along with a few other things. And as you can see these are still self-employment positions that utilize my talents, so I don't have to depend on a job to hire me. I can still do my own thing at my own pace. It's just that these are my talents, not my passion. So, anytime I get in a jam then I can pull one of my trades from under my belt to earn some extra cash until I can get things back on track. These are your side hustles. These are things that you know how to do well but are not your passion, so you don't take them as serious as you would take your passion. When you are an entrepreneur you have to have a plan A, B, C, and D because in the work world people plan for success, but in the entrepreneur world you have to plan for failure before you plan for success. You have to make sure you have a bulletproof plan all the way around the board. You never want to put yourself in a situation where you start to panic because you will not be able to make sound decisions. I've been there and done that and it almost drove me crazy. I'm so glad that I learned from my mistakes and am able to pass down my knowledge and experiences to you.

Make sure you have a saving account or two. Learn how to separate your money, such as monthly expenses, business expenses, retirement, miscellaneous expenses, survival money, and spending money for whatever you choose to do and don't dip and dab into other accounts. Leave them alone so they can serve their purpose. To ensure that I have more self-control I use this method. Once I open up a savings account, I don't get the card to that account. You know why? Because if I don't have a card it makes it harder for me to access the money. This will teach you discipline and self-control over your spending habits. A good friend of mine has another effective technique she uses. She puts money into empty water bottles. Every time she breaks a bill, for instance, a ten-dollar bill, she puts the remaining change in there, whether it's a dollar bill or a five-dollar bill. The reason why she uses this method is because once she drops the money in there, she cannot get it out because the opening hole is too small and the only way to get the money is to break the bottle. So, she uses this as her last resort if she really needs the money! Imagine how much you could save in a year! Find a technique that works best for you and stick to it.

A lot of people know how to make money but don't know how to keep or manage it once they get it. I was once guilty of this myself. That's why a lot of people have poor spending habits and never know where their money is going. Don't be that kind of person. You work hard every day for your money so you should know where it is going, and you should know how to control your money so your money isn't controlling you for the rest of your life. And what I mean by that is when it starts to go out faster than it is comes in, forcing you further away from your goals, making you work extra hard. "Save money and money will save you." get a grip on your money and know where it is going. Now that you have your mind straight, you know the dos and don'ts when trying to be a successful entrepreneur. Now it's time to set your goals in stone. It's time to make your path official and put it in black and white.

CHAPTER 13

GOAL SETTING

"A goal without a plan is just a wish."

Grab a pen and paper. It's about to get real but fun. You are getting ready to build your empire from scratch! Are you ready? By the time we are done with this chapter you will know the importance of goal setting, but not only that, you will be able to create your own goals and find your passion! Goal setting is the first obstacle that you will face when entering the entrepreneur world. I'm not going to sugar coat anything. I'm going to give it to you just like it is! A lot of people want to be an entrepreneur but don't know where to start. So, I created something special to teach you how you can reach your goals and make your dreams come true. First, let's break down what a goal is, and the difference between your purpose, talents, and passion that leads to a fountain of cash. Before you can set your goals, you have to first find your passion! What is your passion? A lot of people confuse their talents with their passion and that's why it takes them so long to find their passion. Ask yourself this question, what do you see yourself doing with enjoyment, even if you couldn't get paid for it? What could you see yourself volunteering to do even after you retire? This is how you figure out your passion, which will lead you to your purpose. Pretty simple, right? Talents, on the other hand, are things you do because you know how to do them and have some experience in them. You can also look at a talent as a side hustle. Something you do for some extra cash. For example, I thought being a cosmetologist was my passion because I was loving the money more than the art itself, so after a while it started to make me miserable and drain me, so I just let it go. This caused me to have to go back to the drawing board at square one. This is something that you don't want to do because you can't get wasted time back, so this is where you need to figure out what your passion is versus your talent. My passion is writing. I can write all day, whether I'm happy or sad, whether I'm getting paid or not. This is something that I enjoy because it's a way for me to express how I feel. It's therapeutic for me, as well. Also, it gives me a chance to spread knowledge. This is what give me my drive. So, ask yourself what your passion is.

On a piece of paper write down your talents and passions. Now cross off all your talents. Then go through your passions list and put a star next to the passion that you love the most out of them all. Congratulations! You have just found your passion! Now that we've got that clear your passion will lead you to your purpose in life. A lot of people go through life and never understand their purpose in life. We were all born with a purpose in life. It is up to us to discover it. For me, writing, which is my passion, led me to my purpose, which is being an author and teacher. Nothing brings me more satisfaction than knowing I made a difference in someone's life and have the wisdom to help others change their whole mindset. I love to create leaders, not followers. That's when your profit fountain will come pouring in like you never expected it to. Your passion is the only thing that you will put your all into, your blood, sweat, and tears, with the least stress but the most enjoyment. Now on the flip side, I am not saying that you can't pursue your talents because again, you can do anything you put your mind too. All I'm saying is that first you must define your passion and know how to differentiate it from the others. Again, talents are a side hustle, so that's a lane that you can jump into once you have established your passion. These can also be the small goals that can lead up into the main goal, which is your end result. It all depends on how you set your goals up and what you are trying to achieve.

Before going any further let's define what a goal is. "A goal is an idea of the future or desired result that a person or a group of people envisions, plans, and commits to achieve." In other words, a goal is the blueprint of all your dreams. It is a blueprint of which direction you want to go and how you are going to get there. Food comes with preparation instructions in order to make the dish so that it comes out exactly how it appears on the front of the box. It's the same for goal setting. Goal setting is your instructions on what and how you plan on succeeding in life and how you picture your life to be. Goals are things that you plan on accomplishing in your lifetime. Basically, they are a plan that outlines your actions in order to get certain results. You should always have short term and long-term goals and your short-term goals should lead you right to your long-term goals. By now I know you are ready to set your goals in stone.

Have you ever heard of S.M.A.R.T. goals? S.M.A.R.T. goals help you not only set your goals but also monitor your performance while reaching your goals. This method is very effective. Many entrepreneurs use this method, and this is what you call the baby stages of building your empire. Each letter of the S.M.A.R.T. goals is an abbreviation for a word and is a main ingredient to effectively planning and plotting your goals. The S stands for "specific." All your goals should be specific, and this is the goal are you trying to accomplish, why you want to accomplish this, and how are you going to accomplish this part of your goal. The M stands for "measurable." Are your goals measurable? Are you giving yourself enough space to execute your goals? The A stands for "achievable." Are your goals achievable? Are they realistic? Do you have the experience, skills, finances, and resources to achieve this goal? Is the risk lower than the reward? What will completing this goal cost you? Meaning what sacrifices will you have to make to complete this goal. This is where you have to decide how big or small your goal is and the in between steps it will take to accomplish your goal to determine if it is achievable. The R stands for "results." What results will come from completing your goals? What will be the outcome from this completed goal? The T stands for "time." Every goal you create should have a deadline. Now I'm not saying that it has to have an exact date, but there should be some type of deadline. Sometimes when we put exact deadlines on something it puts extra pressure on us, and when we don't meet that deadline, discouragement can set in and we may panic or becomes less motivated because we feel like we've failed. So, even if you don't want to do an exact date, do it by month or year and work on it like that until you learn your speed and are comfortable enough to set the exact deadline. For example, for someone who plans on launching a clothing line, their S.M.A.R.T. goal may look like this: "By September 15, 2019 or by September, 2019 ABC clothing Inc. plans on launching plus size clothing to ensure we are reaching all markets, including plus size consumers. We plan on launching the sweat suits first, and the first completed sample must be done June, 2019 to allow the company enough time to fix any imperfections. ABC Clothing Inc. will be having these items manufactured in Kansas to ensure mass production and ensure the budget per unit is under $10."

Do you see how I broke down that S.M.A.R.T. goal and answered all the questions that each abbreviation stands for? Now that is effective goal planning. Make sure you follow these steps whenever you are goal setting. Because anyone can have goals but what good are goals without an accurate plan? Are you ready to start setting your goals? I created an outline to better help you set your goals. You can also go on Google or any other search engine and print out some blank S.M.A.R.T goals template worksheets. I suggest getting a binder and using subject dividers to label each goal. Your goals should be broken down into time frames. Start with your six months goals, then one-year goals, then two-year goals, then five and ten-year goals. This binder will keep your goals organized and all in one place. You can always add, remove, or file things away as needed. Each goal gets their own individual section. Then proceed to do the S.M.A.R.T. goal process. This is the most important to ensure your goals are met.

After creating a solid goal, write down each step that it will take to complete that goal. They don't have to be in order at this point. Just get them down on the paper. After you are completely sure you have all the steps you need to complete this goal. Then go thru your list and next to each task mark it with a number in order according to what is to get completed first to last. This will make sure you don't skip a step and also shows you the steps until completion. Once you get your goals down pat, I'm going to show you a little trick that will make your life even easier. This step will help you see where your goal currently is, and how far you have to go until the finish line. You are going to create a timeline for each goal. This will paint a picture to help you visualize your process because sometimes when we see things and have something to physically look at, it keeps us motivated and focused and it also lets us see your progress. When we don't see our progress at times we tend to slack because we don't see the growth of our goals and don't see how much each little step counts.

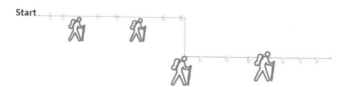

This is how your timeline should look or something similar to this. It should show all the steps broken down, starting from the main steps, which are the images of the person walking, and then the main steps broken down into smaller steps, which are the yellow lines. So, each big step gets completed and helps you move right along in your path. Do you see how this method lets you see your development and where you stand along your journey? Let's do an example to make sure you really have it down pat. Let's say you wanted to open a hair salon. The images of the person walking would be the main steps, for example, "get cosmetology license", "get business license", "find building/location, and "buy supplies." The yellow lines would represent the steps to complete each larger step, for instance, the first large step is to obtain a cosmetology license before you can do anything. What steps do you have to take to get your cosmetology license? You have to find a school of your preference that offers such license, you have to get funding, you have to finish up classes. Then move on to the next blue major step and figure out what smaller steps you have to take to complete that step. Pretty cool! Something so simple could be a game changer for the better. Creating a map or timeline for each goal is very important because as you can see it allows you to see the direction you are going; see how far you are from the finish line. When you want to give up you should look at your goal map because this will inspire you to keep going. This method is very effective. I use this method for my personal and business goals I swear by this method. This method will simplify any goal, especially a challenging and complicated one. This is a good way to break it down. Once you have this method down pat, goal setting and executing them will be second nature to you.

Also, another thing that you can incorporate into your goal setting process after you map everything out is to create a visionary board this is very effective and can help you visualize what your goals and dream will look like once you complete them. What is a visionary board? A visionary board is a board that displays all your images of whatever you want to accomplish in life. This is a good idea because sometimes when you see your ideas it helps motivate you and helps you to keep pushing forward. Let me give you an example. Say your dream was to own your own hair salon then you would get a poster board or tri-fold board and, get some magazines or pictures from offline that show how you would want your hair salon to look from the outside in. Do you see where I'm going with this? Now that you have a physical picture of your dream salon this will help you to keep moving forward with your goals. You can incorporate all your goals in the visionary board and include everything you want to do or have in life. For example, on my visionary board I included my dream house, car, family, and business that I want to own. I even included how I want my dream wedding to be. I even included my dream vacation for instance a tropical island, and I got a picture of myself that I placed on the picture with me on the beach. Your visionary board can be anyway you make it. This just an overview look at your future. So, again, during times when you feel like giving up, take a look at your visionary board and ask yourself if you really to give up. Look what future you will be giving up on! I love visionary boards because they give you a chance to daydream about your future and remind yourself why you are working so hard. Once you are done you can place it on the wall or any place where you spend a lot of your time. You can check out sample visionary boards to get some ideas for how you want to create yours. Also, you can look for local visionary board gatherings because visionary boards are becoming more popular, so a lot of people hold social gatherings to do them. I have been to one before and it was fun. The settings are different, but most will have light food, wine, supplies, and good energy. You will be around people who are trying to do what you are trying to do so this is a great way to network and exchange ideas.

Now how are you feeling? Are you feeling more comfortable and confident to enter the entrepreneur spirit? If you still a little unsure ask yourself why. Make a list of what's making you unsure and revisit that topic. "Anything that works against you can also work for you once you understand the principle of reverse." -Maya Angelou

So now that you are equipped with the right tools needed to be the best version of yourself, let's jump into the right tools needed for your business to thrive. In the next chapter you will be able to create your own business plan. This is the exciting part because this is the birth of your baby AKA your business venture.

CHAPTER 14

BUSINESS PLAN

"If the plan doesn't work change the plan, not the goal."

Congratulations! We are almost at the end and we are knocking down those brick walls that once stood in your way, slowly but surely, and creating a new path for you to achieve greatness. What is a business plan and why is it so important? A business plan is information pertaining to your business venture. It outlines the what, when, and how your business will fit in the economy. It shows the niche of the company, and forecasting of the business and the future plans and growth. In simpler words, look at a business plan as a story about your business from the very beginning to the very end of the business. Business plans are also important because they will guide the company along the path. Without a business plan you will not be able to secure a business loan. I mean, would you lend thousands of dollars to someone if they did not have a solid plan for how they would pay you back? That is how the banks look at it. They want to see why they should lend your business this loan. They have to make sure that the business will be a success and will be able to pay back the loan. Even if you do not want funding for your business, a business plan is a must because it will show the direction of the company and make sure everyone is on the same page and moving in one direction. How can a company be successful if you don't know where your company stands? You will not be able to know the direction the company will take. In addition, business plans are important because they allow you to see when the company is starting to go left and fix any obstacles that get in the way. Business plans are a blueprint of your business venture.

Business plan writing may not be as fun as you think but it forces you to do four things. It helps motivate others and get them excited about joining the team. It helps you figure out your company's unique qualities.

It helps keep you focused and keep your eyes on the prize. Lastly, it helps you set goals, which we already discussed in the previous chapter. What we are going to do is break down the most important components of a business plan. Now the good thing about business plan writing is that you can attend workshops and seminars that will assist you in business plan writing to ensure you have a solid plan. But first let's get a clear understanding of the different parts of a business plan and how to effectively create one. By now you should be giving yourself a pat on the back because you are about to create your very own business plan!

A business plan is a written description of every part of your business from the goals, to the business team, to the finance department, and even the obstacles of the company. There are eight key components in a business plan that are very important to understand. This is where you will also figure out how strong or weak your company is and again, where your company fits in the business world.

Executive summary is the first part of the business plan. This is an overall summary of your company. This part of the business plan is usually 1-2 pages. You don't have to overdo this part. Let the facts speak for themselves. Also, when doing a business plan, only put in facts. There should never be assumptions; that would be setting yourself and your business up for failure before it even gets a chance to make it in the marketplace. Your business plan will be a reflection of how well you know your company as well as the industry that you are stepping into. Your executive summary, even though it is the first part of your business plan, should be completed last, so you can include all the accurate details which you won't know until you complete the whole business plan. The executive summary is a pitch of your whole company. Look at your executive summary as if you were trying to gain a potential client. How would you explain your company to them? It should include all the important information about your business. This is where you should include your niche and a summary of all the components of your business. Your executive summary is your five-minute elevator pitch. It should include the company background, market opportunity, advantages over competitors, and financial highlights. Look at the executive summary as a synopsis of your business plan.

Business description/product and services is the part where you describe your company and what your company offers, such as your products and/or services, and whether or not it is a new or existing company. This is where you include your mission statement. Your mission statement is the purpose of your business and is usually only a few short sentences. For example, the American Diabetes Association's mission statement is "To prevent and cure diabetes and to improve the lives of all people affected by diabetes." Pretty simple and straight to the point. Now, ask yourself what is your company mission statement? What purpose is your company trying to fulfill with your consumers? When doing your company description make sure you include the present state and the future possibilities of the industry in which you are in. Make sure you have reliable data to back up anything that you are saying because this is what investors and banks look at when putting their money into a project. Also, you can include any new projects or developments that will not only benefit your company but could be a challenge to your company as well, such as milestones and obstacles. Be sure to include your manufacturing process, availability of materials, how you handle inventory and fulfillment, and all other operational details. This is where you can include a little background history of the company and how it was formed. This is where you get into a little more detail. You should describe the company's location and legal structure, such as Limited Liability Company (LLC), Limited Partnership (LP), Sole Proprietor, etc. You should also include the company's core principles and financial resources. Describe the projected growth and some of the market opportunities as well as various aspects of your servicing offering and the history and current happenings of your field. This section is the backbone of your company and sets the stage for the rest of the information included in the rest of the business plan. This is where you include how your business is different from competitors. You can keep this short by describing the industry in one paragraph, the product or service in another one, and 3-4 paragraphs describing the business and its success. This is a great way to end this part of the business plan.

Market analysis and research is where you can look at your competitors and what they have over you and your advantage over them. This will determine your place in the market. This is where you will also describe your target market, including profiles of your ideal customers and their background, as well as trends of the industry that you are in.

Sales forecast is where you can include testimonials. There's nothing like having other people's feedback, especially from current customers. This is where you describe pricing and distribution and the future of your business. A great way to begin this is by describing the market size, structure, growth prospects, trends, and potential sales. Also, research and include the sales information of your competitors to determine the total potential market.

Organization and management is the part where you get to introduce your management team and their roles in the company. This part of the plan is critical because when securing financing they look at your team members to ensure you have the right team with the right skills to ensure the successful direction of the business. This is where you can highlight your business team's skills, backgrounds, and areas of expertise. Also, include how your management team will help you meet the company goals. This is what investors and banks look at when determining the risk of the company to see if the management team will be strong enough for the company's growth and success. A solid, experienced, and knowledgeable management team lowers the risk of the company. They want to make sure you have the right staff to run and direct the company to be successful enough for them to get their investment returns. This is the part that will either get venture capitalists' and banks' attention or make them call off the deal. Your organization and management team are everything. This could be your deal breaker. So, make sure you have the right players on your team to carry out the mission of the company.

Sales strategies is where you explain how you will generate profits from the company and where you talk about the company's pricing strategy. This is also where you will explain the company's promotional strategies and how the company plans or utilizing it. How does the company plan on raising brand awareness such as press releases, social media, etc?

Funding requirements is where you will be describing the amount of funding you need to either get your business off the ground or grow your existing business. This is where facts have to come in. You have to be accurate and honest when money comes in to play. You don't want to under-predict and over-predict the numbers. You must be 100% accurate because this is where the plan will go as planned or this is where you could stumble upon a pothole. The plan is to seal the deal, not destroy the deal so make sure all your ducks are lined up and you know how much you need to borrow and for what. What will this funding do for your business? How will such funding benefit your company? You must be able to show how much financial backing you need to get your business to the next level.

Financial summary is where you include projections, your profit and loss statements, balance sheets, and cash flow statements for the next 3-5 years. This is your accounting details for future projects, not current ones. This is where you will forecast the future of your business. The financial projections section is also where you include your revenue growth and trends of the company. This is very important, especially if you are doing an expansion of your existing company. This is where you also discuss the return on the investments. You can do a timeline projection, so investors know what and when to expect their returns from the company. Breakdown the profit margin of the company and project future profits of the company. To better put this, the financial summary is where you provide numbers to back up everything you were saying in the other components of the business plan. You want to take what and where your company currently is, combined with sales strategies, to create realistic projections. Calculate when investors can expect their returns and when you will break even. That sums up the key components of the business plan.

Although, there are other parts of the business plan, those are the main components that you, your business team, and investors look at to get insight into the company and how strong it is, or if it is ready to enter the marketplace. So whenever starting a business, please ensure that you did your homework and have created a solid business plan. Being an entrepreneur is hard enough, right? So why start a business and put your all into it without even knowing what direction your business will go in, or if it is even strong enough to compete in the business world? Business plans are always good to do when starting a business because they give you a sense of ease. There's nothing like knowing the end result of all your hard work. That's just like taking a road trip to a new country or state that you've never been to. Are you going to just drive, not knowing how you are going to get there? Are you going to guess the routes that you should be taking? Or are you going get a map so you can know for a fact if you take the path outlined in the map it will land you at your intended destination? That's how you should look at a business plan. If you create it right and follow the path of your business plan then you will get your company to the destination that you planned, which is in the marketplace thriving and being successful. Also, if you are still having trouble creating your business plan you can go to your search engine such and search "sample business plans" to get a better idea. I just wanted to break down the main components to give you some type of idea what to do and look forward to, and what should be included in the business plan to ensure you are off to a good start. You can go to the Small Business Administration (SBA) or the S.C.O.R.E. website. They will guide you along your journey and can also help with securing loans, grants, etc. So, use programs like this to your advantage because they were created to help small business owners. The people that assist you are retired executives of all types of business backgrounds, such as CEOs, lawyers, successful entrepreneurs, accountants, etc. They volunteer their services to ensure small business have the right tools, resources, and funding to make sure their business risk is lowered. As far as funding you would have to visit their website to see their requirements, but this is a great resource for your business to use as a tool, so make sure you check into that and use it to your advantage. Now it's time to launch your business!

Level Up: Entrepreneur Spirit Blueprint

CHAPTER 15

LAUNCHING YOUR BUSINESS

"Think big, start small, begin now."

Are you ready for the world to see all your hard work? You should be. This is the happiest but scariest moment of your life, so get ready. This is where you will see how the world will react to all the blood, sweat, and tears that you put into your company. So, make sure when you present your company to the world you are 150% ready because from this point forward there will be no turning back. I always say there's no half doing anything. If you can't do it right, then don't do it at all. And, make sure you are moving at your own pace and are comfortable with where you stand in the business world. Don't let anybody force you to step into the entrepreneur world if you are not ready. I remember when I wrote my first book people kept asking me *when are you going to release it? When is your book coming out? Can I just get a copy now or a sample of it?* All I used to say was that it is was coming soon and that greatness can't be rushed. Make sure your team is ready, as well. Make sure everyone is moving at the same pace. I can't stress this enough. The worst thing you can do is launch your business without it being ready. For one, you are giving your competitors an advantage to fill in your weakness within your company, and it can quickly become their strength and then all your hard work will be out the window. Not only that, but you want your potential and current consumers to know you are serious, strong, and ready for the world. Once you show the world that your company is not strong enough this can tarnish your company image. You can have a great product and have top quality but if you present it wrong or prematurely this could crush your company

In addition, before you announce your business make sure that you have all the legal documentation protecting your company, such as trademark, copyright, patent, whenever you need to do so no one can steal your ideas. Do you know how many people started a great company but didn't protect it properly, so it became someone else's? Don't fall victim to that when all you have to do is take the proper steps to protect your company. It may be a little costly depending on your budget, but if you cannot afford to protect your company, you can always do a poor man's copyright. Now, I'm not saying this will help you win if you have to bring a lawsuit against someone for stealing your ideas, but this may give you some type of lead way because it shows when you established your business. It is always wise to do a poor man's copyright until you can afford to legally do it. And, make sure if you have to do a poor man's copyright, the first chance you get, you do it the legal way. To do a poor man's copywrite all you have to do is type or write up a description of your company, when you established it, and any important information describing your company. Then you mail it to yourself and file it away. Never, I repeat never, open the envelope because on the envelope it is postmarked, so if you have to present it to the judge then the judge will see the postmarked date, which the court can open to review the details and established date that you started your company. This is an inexpensive way to protect your company that will literally cost you nothing. I had to do this before with one of my businesses. Furthermore, when trying to get your company patented or trademarked, it could take months or over a year. Again, a poor man's copyright could cover you until you can do it legally. But whatever you do, make sure your business is protected. Also, make sure that you have your company's website up and running. Set up all your social media accounts. Make sure you have your business cards ready, and keep all your business stuff, such as accounts, social media, website, phones, etc., separate from your personal stuff. It just looks so much more professional, especially when you are a fresh business owner/entrepreneur. People will already have their eyebrows raised waiting for you to slip up, so leave no room for any mistakes.

Another outlet you can use to see if your business is ready for the world find a focus group. What a focus group does is give you feedback on your products or services. This is a method that recording artists use. They perform a song behind a two-way glass. The artist does not see the people behind the glass, but the people giving feedback see the artist. The focus group judges the artist's music, their sound, their image, their lyrics, and determines whether the song and artist are good enough to put out into the market. You can utilize this step to tell you where your business stands before presenting it to the world. It gives you a chance to tweak any areas that may need it. You can also ask friends and family members, but I don't recommend asking only family members because sometimes they will tell you it's a prefect product or service because they don't want to discourage you or hurt your feelings. I prefer focus groups because there is no relationship between you and them, and they can feel free to give their honest feedback. Also, they are potential clients. "There will be obstacles, there will be doubters, there will be mistakes, but with hard work there will no limits."

You are now at the end of the tunnel and I know you see the bright light waiting for you to arrive. But before you reach the light this is where your strength will be tested. This is where you have to be ready to be built Ford tough. This is where all your hard work will have to stand the test of time. This is where all your battles will begin, and where you will fight like never before for your place in the entrepreneur world. This is where you will prove that you deserve to be successful. This is the part where you will either reach your breakdown or break though. This is where your biggest battles will be fought. This is where you just want to throw in the towel and call it quits. You will have to keep fighting to your very last breath. Only the strong survive and make it to the top. And, I believe by this point you ready to take on the world, but there is one more important subject that we must discuss.

CHAPTER 16

BE AWARE: THEY ARE OUT THERE

"Don't lower your expectations to fit into the world. You were born to stand out."

I want to touch on how important self-love is because before you can pursue anything or love anything you must love yourself first. Make sure to always adopt good morals and principles to be the best version of yourself and do it with integrity. Never settle and know your worth because once you settle then you will settle your whole life. Demand what you want when entering the battlefield. Not everyone will play fair in the business world. It can get tricky so make sure you watch out. Just because you may be a stand-up person don't expect everyone to have the same morals and intentions, especially when you are new to the business world. I'm not saying this to scare you because you are supposed to be fearless no matter what, but I just want you to be aware of what you are walking into at all times. And, don't think that just because a person seems like they are good and legit that they really are. How many times did you hear about famous singers getting run over and going broke because they believed in their managers, etc. They trusted the wrong people and ended up going broke because they trusted them so much that they weren't even paying attention to how they were robbing them blind and getting over on them. That's why I always preach that knowledge is power. The more knowledge you have the more power you will have to fight on the battlefield of the business world. Never think you are safe in the business world because you are not. You are swimming with sharks and, unfortunately, we live in a world where the strong prey on the weak, so never show any signs of weakness. Never sign anything unless you have a lawyer. Don't do anything without legal advice. The first two people you better have on your team should be a lawyer and an accountant because they will make sure no one will get over on you, and they will make sure your assets are protected and secure. I have seen so many people get ruined because they put too much trust into the business world. Don't fall victim to that. Protect yourself and follow your instincts. Remember that they will not steer you wrong so follow your gut feeling, no matter what.

Never take anyone's word. Make sure that for any agreements that are made, they are signed and written in black and white, so you can always have something to back you up in case you run into a situation. This is business and when money is involved things can always go left and money can bring out the worst in people, especially when greed is involved. All I'm saying is stay ten steps ahead and on point at all times. I'm not saying to look at everyone as a snake in a suit, but you have to know that snakes do exist and sometimes you won't see it coming. Put your game face on and let them know you came to play no games, because the business world will eat you alive and spit you right back out for the next person to finish you. That's why having a professional team is critical, and even with your team members make sure you know who is on your ship. If not, you will walk away with the short end of the stick ready to kill somebody. So, to avoid that, prepare yourself and understand everything that sounds good isn't good. I know you have heard that saying "if it sounds too good to be true then it usually is" so take heed to that saying and live by it.

Never let anybody sell you a dream. Do your research on people. Know their background and find out what type of person they are for the most part. In addition, never move at someone else's pace and never depend on someone else to get your foot in the door. You have to work hard until one day your work makes so much noise that the world has no choice but to pay attention. You can't depend on anyone to get you to the top. It just doesn't work like that. I cringe when I hear people say it's not about what you know, it's about who you know. There is some truth to that but even if you know someone who is already successful and can help further your career, will still have to bring something to the table besides, *I know such and such.* You might get your 15 minutes of fame, but how far do you think that is going to take you? You can't use that forever. Never allow someone to spoon feed you. That's another sign of weakness. You should always surround yourself with people who teach you how to fish verses spoon feeding you. What I mean by that is never settle for breadcrumbs when you can learn how to bake your own loaf of bread and eat forever. There are people out here that need their ego stroked so they try to keep people below them because they are really weak. Don't fall for that trap either. Just know you can be the sweetest person in the world, but you still have to be assertive at the same time. Don't let anybody get over on you. You may have to turn down plenty of opportunities. Don't jump at the first sight or else you could end up being a meal for all the business vultures that are walking around. To be honest, the business world can be worse than the drug game; they just don't use guns and drugs, they use suit and ties, contracts, their knowledge, and take it and run with it. So be aware and boss up on whoever you must. Show them there is nothing weak about you. Never mix business with pleasure. That's a disaster waiting to happen. If its business, keep it business. Always keep the two separated as much as possible and make sure that you demand respect. I don't care who it is. Make sure they treat you with the highest level of respect. If not, remove yourself from that circle and let karma deal with the rest.

CHAPTER 17

FAREWELL: SEE YOU AT THE TOP!

"Walk this journey with faith and you will reach your destiny."

Unfortunately, it is time to say our goodbyes. It was a pleasure writing this book and passing down my wisdom and knowledge to help ease your journey as you walk into the entrepreneur spirit. I wish you nothing but the best and I hope everything that you ever wanted in life comes your way. Just remember, never lose your faith, always believe in yourself, and believe that you are capable of achieving whatever you put your mind to do. "The key to unlock your entrepreneur spirit is your imagination." Never stop dreaming, never stop chasing your goals, and never give up no matter what obstacles you are facing. No matter what, make sure you stay true to yourself and walk your own journey. Don't ever let anyone create your destiny for you and remember, "failure is an event, not a person" -Zig Zag

You can't help anyone until you can help yourself, but make sure when you are in a better predicament to help others you reach your leading hand out to pull others in; that's the only way you will receive your blessing. It's lonely at the top when you're by yourself so never be selfish. There's enough room for everyone to win. And, never step on anybody's toes. You will get your turn. Just be patient. Every entrepreneur has a story to tell about their journey to the top. Enjoy the ups and downs because the ups are where you celebrate your achievements, but the downs are where you learn lessons to carry you to the next level in your journey and mold you into a warrior. Accept all failures. They are beautiful lessons. Entrepreneurship is not for everyone as you just learned. I conducted interviews with several entrepreneurs who fought their way through it and came out on top. They have a special message for you as they share their point of view and challenges that they faced along their journey of entrepreneurship. Just some extra fuel for when you're running low on gas. This is what they had to say:

SHELLY WILLIAMS, PHILLY'S O.P.R.A.H.

How long have you been an entrepreneur?

I am most known for hosting the segment, *Word on the Street* on Urban X-pressions but what most people don't know is that I am also one of the executive producers of Urban X-pressions, a three-time Billboard award winning show and the longest running video show in Philadelphia broadcast history featuring music videos, celebrity guests, and community leaders. In 1999, I decided to quit my job as the executive assistant to Dorothy E. Brunson, General Manager of WGTW TV 48 to be a full-time producer of Urban X-pressions. Dorothy E. Brunson was the first African American woman to own a television station and with her blessings and mentoring, I felt confident to move forward to be an entrepreneur. However, from 2013 to 2016 I took a position in the corporate offices of Forman Mills as a creative/social media manager and community relations. It was definitely an offer that I couldn't refuse. I didn't give up on my entrepreneur endeavors while employed; I continued producing my talk show *Single on a Saturday Night*.

What's the name of your business and what product or service do you provide?

I am the President and CEO of X-pressions, Incorporated, which is a nonprofit media and mentoring program. I would consider myself to be a serial entrepreneur, with experience in a multitude of areas and have been described by many business associates and friends as Philly's O.P.R.A.H. I am a three-time Billboard Award winning television producer, creative manager, social media manager, certified notary signing agent, TV host, philanthropist, speaker, columnist for Scoop USA Newspaper and What's Happening Philly, and I work in advertising sales.

X-pressions, Inc. a non-profit media program that produces *Single On A*

Saturday Night, dedicated to using the power of talk therapy and visual media to serve diverse populations through our monthly group talk therapy sessions, sexual health training courses, and quality programming intended to foster education and inspire healthy relationships. (Xpressionsinc.net) (SingleOnSaturdayNite.com)

What advice would you give someone who wants to become an entrepreneur?

Believe in yourself, be consistent, create multiple streams of income, read, study, listen, build strong relationships, know your worth and value. When it gets hard, don't give up. Success is not determined by your wealth. Build a strong team. Trust God and know that He has a plan to prosper you. Nothing is too hard for God.

What are some of the challenges that you faced along your journey?

Challenge 1: Balance, since I'm working on several different projects, I find it a challenge sometimes to find balance.

Challenge 2: Making sure I stay relevant in an ever-changing society. I started out on a very successful television show, *Urban X-pressions*, which aired from 1992-2013 on broadcast TV. Now that we are in the digital/internet space I continue to look for ways to stay relevant.

Challenge 3: Creating a steady flow of income. The bulk of what I do is entertainment and to fund some of the TV shows you need sponsors. I found that when you are on top people call you, and when you are building something new the same people aren't as receptive, but I understand that it is business. I could go on and on about challenges because there will always be challenges, but it's what you do with the challenges that makes a difference. In spite of any challenge I will not give up.

ROBERT J. WHEELER

I am the co-owner of Truth Philly Nightclub and have over 20 years as an entrepreneur. My first business was a takeout seafood restaurant. Some advice I would give an upcoming entrepreneur would be find a mentor, be willing to work long hours. Be okay with filing all positions at first. Make a business plan. Some challenges I faced were not having enough money. You need capital to help grow your business. Also, lack of support from family and friends, and marketing and promotion. One of my favorite quotes is "To think you're supposed to win all the time is a loser's mentality!" You have to be prepared to lose nine times for the one time that's worth it all.

JOSHUA "JAY RIVERS"

I have been an entrepreneur since 2005. I am best known as an author, writer, and lyricist. My business name is J. Rivers Enterprise LLC. I provide/promote literary works and music entertainment and services that are designed to uplift the human spirit. Advice I would give is to have a thorough plan, one with deadlines, goals, and objectives, and develop thick skin. Being an entrepreneur is tough and it's filled with a lot of nos, disappointments, and financial expenses that you won't recoup immediately. But keep believing in yourself. Put the work in, and the results will come, and stay away from "yes men" who will blind you. Another challenge I faced was believing in myself. I started out without a blueprint and very little support, especially financially. It's hard to believe in something only you can see. One of my favorite quotes is "Your best life is waiting on the other side of fear."

CHARLES G. SMITH, JR.

I have been an entrepreneur since 1997. On Da Chace LLC provides photography, graphic design, mixology, videography, and management services. Some advice I would give is to look forward to failing. That's the only way you're going to learn and prosper. To be successful in your own business you must learn to accept failure and look to invest in yourself rather than wait for others. Some of the challenges I faced were trying to please others while I wasn't happy with myself and at a standstill, and not developing until I learned that you cannot please everyone in life. You have to do what truly makes you happy because that person isn't trying to reciprocate; if they were you both or all would be in a better state than what you are in now. Also, dealing with the process of getting all the paperwork together. The city, state, and government want to know everything inside out. My favorite quote is "Be On Da Chace and Chace your dreams."

Now that you have some insight from some top entrepreneurs who have been in the game for a while you know what to look forward to. Now the whole twist to be an entrepreneur is that it can be a smooth journey with a few bumps along the way or it can be a rough journey that can turn into your worst nightmare. When you have the right armor, you stand a chance against anything, so I hope you enjoyed the suit of armor that I made for you. Now it's time to gear up, grab your sword, and chase your dreams full throttle. Don't let anything or anyone get in your way. I have one last surprise for you to give you something to think about. Turn the page. This is the last piece to the puzzle. Farewell to all my future entrepreneurs. I can't wait to hear all about your journey. I am patiently waiting and rooting for you. Until next time, be your biggest cheerleader and stay true to yourself no matter what.

BONUS: CHAPTER 18

STRUGGLE

"Struggle is meant to groom you for who you are meant to be."

Dear Struggle,

Struggle, I know you thought I forgot about you but how could I forget about MY GREATEST TEACHER OF ALL TIME? Struggle, you have seen me cry, fight, and hold on for dear life. You've seen me at the top and clapped and seen me at the bottom picking me up. I never got a chance to tell you this, Struggle, but you gave me the strength that I have today and that's why I will never give up. Thank you. Because of you I am now considered a threat, but I know what you will say. I can hear it now: "Vita Ann, stay humble and walk with grace" and because of you that's just what I am going to do. Because of you I can now walk with my head held high. Because of you my tears are no longer fears. The biggest lesson that you taught me was that happiness only sneaks in a door that you did not think could open, because never in a million years did I think my happiness was on the other side of your door. You taught me that it is not about the setback, it is about the get back. People are so worried about the drawback that they cannot see their own comeback. That's why after thinking about it and opening my eyes I never had to backtrack. Even when it felt like I was, it was just a sidetrack, you know, a distraction testing me to see if I was ready to give the world it's payback. I remember when I was stuck at the bus stop you were talking to me and you told me "be patient… your way out is your 11th finger, which is your pen. One day the world will see the weight you carried on your shoulders." We have been on one hell of a journey. Struggle. Boy, oh boy, if only they knew half of our stories. I'm just happy that we can now look back at it and laugh. "The harder the struggle the more glorious the triumph. To be continued…✐

ACKNOWLEDGEMENTS

To the man above, Father God, here we are once again, and all praise goes to you because without you I am nothing. For so many years I questioned my reasons on this earth, and all you kept telling me was to walk in your shadow and one day soon you would reveal it to me. Father God, thank you once again for showing me that you will never leave my side and that victory belongs to me. I am so thankful and grateful for every single blessing that you sent my way. I am thankful and blessed for being gifted in such a talent that I will be able to change the world. Time after time you protected and shielded me so I could be limitless. How can I ever repay you for being such a loving and caring god? I know I am far from perfect and have made plenty of mistakes, but you showed me that anything is possible as long as I never question your power. You showed me that every saint has a past, and every sinner has a future. Father God, thank you for allowing me to complete another mission.

All I ask is that you continue to guide me in the right path allow me to continue to walk into greatness. Father God, you deserve so much more credit than what is given to you.

My four kings, Mommy did it again, I know walking this journey has not been easy and I know there's a lot that you may not understand, but the only thing that I what you to know is everything that I do is for you all. I want to wake up and see my four kings without a worry in the world. I want you to know that you were raised by a real queen. I want you to know that after every storm the rainbow will come out for sure. All you have to do is be patient and you will see.

SHYHEED, my oldest king, you are everything I ever dreamed of. From your humbled spirit to your leadership skills to you knowing that giving up is not an option. Son, I am so proud of you and at times I ask God what I did to deserve such an amazing son like you. I know your future is bright, not only because you have my blood running through you, but because you are curious. You never stop learning and you are a trendsetter. You have more wisdom than a little bit. I appreciate you in so many ways. There were times when I had to turn to you for encouragement. Son, all I can say is keep shining bright like you already are doing, and greatness awaits you. Continue to be fearless no matter what because Mommy will always be right there to catch you.

JAINEALL, my second oldest king and future football player. Mr. Know it All. You have big dreams already my math genius. Son, keep striving and being curious about life and soon you will find all the answers that you search for, and I will be right there in your shadow making sure you don't take any wrong detours. I see your inner entrepreneurial traits peeking out already at such an early age and I am forever proud of your drive and hunger to always want to know more.

JAMILL, my little miracle king, son, you have more than a little bit of potential, All you dream about is being a pilot and I will do everything in my power to make sure your dream comes true. I want you to continue to be my honor student with big dreams, and one day you won't just be a pilot, you will have your own pilot. Yes, we are speaking it into existence because I know it will happen.

JAMIR, you just leave a sparkle wherever you go. You have a personality that just shines effortlessly, Baby Boy. I hope you get everything you want to get out of life. I know your dream is to be an actor and with your personality I don't see how that would ever be a problem. I know Hollywood better watch out because they have one hell of an actor to look forward to. Mommy will make sure of it. Your wish is my command.

Mommy loves all of you and I hope that I make you all proud as I continue to pave the way to a better life for us all. What makes our bond so special is that I never walked this journey alone. You were by my side through it all. Not many people can be a full-time mother and entrepreneur and continue to chase dreams with their kids attached to them. This journey wouldn't be special if I couldn't walk it with you. just know it takes a special kind of queen to do what Mommy has done. We grind together and we will shine together as one.

Thank you to all my family and supporters. There are too many to name, but it definitely didn't go unnoticed and you know who you are. No need to explain. I am forever grateful to have such great supporters and people that want to see me genuinely survive and thrive in the game of life.

Made in the USA
Columbia, SC
26 November 2024

47210635R00119